The College Experience Compact

Amy Baldwin

Pulaski Technical College

Brian Tietje

California Polytechnic State University, San Luis Obispo

Boston · Columbus · Indianapolis · New York · San Francisco · Upper Saddle River
Amsterdam · Cape Town · Dubai · London · Madrid · Milan · Munich · Paris · Montréal · Toronto
Delhi · Mexico City · São Paulo · Sydney · Hong Kong · Seoul · Singapore · Taipei · Tokyo

Editor-in-Chief: Jodi McPherson
Acquisitions Editor: Katie Mahan
Editorial Assistant: Erin Carreiro
Development Editor: Elana Dolberg
Senior Managing Editor: Karen Wernholm
Senior Author Support/Technology Specialist:
    Joe Vetere
Senior Production Project Manager: Kathleen
    A. Manley
Executive Marketing Manager: Amy Judd

Senior Procurement Specialist: Megan
    Cochran
Image Manager: Rachel Youdelman
Permissions Manager: Cheryl Besenjak
Permissions Project Manager: Pam Foley
Text Design and Production Coordination:
    Electronic Publishing Services Inc.
Composition and Illustration: Jouve
Cover Designer: Diane Lorenzo
Cover Photo: Nata-Lia/Shutterstock

Credits and acknowledgments for material borrowed from other sources and reproduced, with permission, in this textbook appear on the appropriate page within the text.

Photo credits: p. 1: Shutterstock; p. 3: Steveball/Shutterstock; p. 8: Shutterstock; p. 9: Shutterstock; p. 15: Shutterstock; p. 17: Alex Hinds/Shutterstock; p. 21: Marcio Eugenio/Shutterstock; p. 23: Michal Popiel/Shutterstock; p. 27: Shutterstock; p. 28: Rob Marmion/Shutterstock; p. 31: Fotolia; p. 34: Shutterstock; p. 39: Shutterstock; p. 40: Shutterstock; p. 42 (all): Shutterstock; p. 43: Shutterstock; p. 45: Natalia D./Shutterstock; p. 49 (all): Shutterstock; p. 54: Layland Masuda/Shutterstock; p. 56: Shutterstock; p. 58: Shutterstock; p. 61: Shutterstock; p. 62: Alexander Raths/Fotolia; p. 68: Fotolia; p. 69: Tomasz Trojanowski/Shutterstock; p. 73: Shutterstock; p. 74: Suprijono Suharjoto/Fotolia; p. 79: Fotolia; p. 80: Fotolia; p. 83: Shutterstock; p. 84: Ian Shaw/Alamy; p. 86: iStockphoto; p. 90: Frederick Bass/Getty Images; p. 95: Shutterstock; p. 97: Gino Santa Maria/Fotolia; p. 99: Shutterstock; p. 103: Diego Cervo/Fotolia; p. 107: Andresr/Shutterstock; p. 109: Lithian/Fotolia; p. 111: Fotolia; p. 113: Joel Natkin/iStockphoto; p. 117: Shutterstock; p. 119: Vlue/Shutterstock; p. 122: Richard Green/Alamy; p. 124: Justin Sullivan/Getty Images; p. 129: Shutterstock; p. 131: Fotolia; p. 134: RubberBall Productions/Getty Images; p. 137: Fotolia

Many of the designations by manufacturers and sellers to distinguish their products are claimed as trademarks. Where those designations appear in this book, and the publisher was aware of a trademark claim, the designations have been printed in initial caps or all caps.

Library of Congress Cataloging-in-Publication Data

Baldwin, Amy
    The college experience compact / Amy Baldwin, M.A., Pulaski Technical College, Brian Tietje, Ph.D., California Polytechnic State University, San Luis Obispo.
        p. cm.
    Includes bibliographical references and index.
    ISBN-13: 978-0-321-85691-3
    ISBN-10: 0-321-85691-0
    1. College student orientation—United States.   2. College students—Conduct of life.
I. Tietje, Brian C.   II. Title.
    LB2343.32.B2384 2013
    378.1'98—dc23
                                                                        2012038606

1 2 3 4 5 6 7 8 9 10—CRK—16 15 14 13 12

www.pearsonhighered.com

ISBN 10: 0-321-85691-0
ISBN 13: 978-0-321-85691-3

ABOUT THE AUTHORS

AMY BALDWIN is an instructor of writing, literature, and college success at Pulaski Technical College in North Little Rock, Arkansas. Since 1996, she has served the college in various roles, including self-study editor, distance education coordinator, and professional development coordinator. She is also the author of four student success textbooks that were the first on the market to address the special needs of students: The Community College Experience, Brief Edition, third edition (Pearson, 2012), The First-Generation College Experience (Pearson, 2012), The Community College Experience, third edition (Pearson, 2013), and The College Experience (Pearson, 2013). She has also facilitated over 120 workshops and breakout sessions all over the country—at community colleges, K–12 professional days, and national conferences—on teaching and learning issues such as transitioning to college, student engagement practices, and active learning. Amy will complete her doctorate of higher education from the University of Arkansas at Little Rock in December 2012. The focus of her dissertation is student engagement, retention, and success for African American males in college. She is also serving as the project manager for the Complete College America initiative for the state of Arkansas.

BRIAN TIETJE is a professor of marketing and the dean of continuing education at Cal Poly State University, San Luis Obispo. His undergraduate business degree is from Bowling Green State University (1988), his MBA is from the University of Hawaii (1994), and his Ph.D. in marketing is from the University of Washington (1999). Dr. Tietje is passionate about student learning. He has won several teaching awards, is the co-author of Anybody's Business with Barbara Van Syckle, and has authored the Wall Street Journal weekly educator's review for over 10 years. As associate dean at the Orfalea College of Business, he spearheaded efforts to improve student success and graduation rates and led the effort to develop alternative modes of course delivery to improve student learning. He also served as the principal facilitator of the college's assessment of learning program for AACSB accreditation. Brian lives on the central coast of California with his family, friends, and pets.

ACKNOWLEDGMENTS

A very special thank you to the following people for helping me during the process of writing this book: Kyle, Emily, and Will; Jodi McPherson, Katie Mahan, Elana Dolberg, Amy Judd, Charlotte Morrissey, and Erin Carreiro.

—*Amy Baldwin*

Many thanks to Amy, Jodi, Katie, and Elana for allowing me to be part of this exciting program. My heartfelt gratitude also goes to my wife, Debbie, for her encouragement and support throughout this project and my career—I couldn't have done it without you.

—*Brian Tietje*

BRIEF CONTENTS

1   Your Mission Statement and Goals   1

2   Time Management   15

3   Money Management   27

4   Critical and Creative Thinking   39

5   Learning Style Preference   49

6   Listening and Note Taking   61

7   Reading and Note Taking   73

8   Studying and Test Taking   83

9   Communication and Diversity   95

10   Information Literacy   107

11   Managing Stress   117

12   Career Exploration   129

CONTENTS

Preface   ix

Introduction for Faculty   x

Introduction for Students   xii

CHAPTER 1   Your Mission Statement and Goals   1

Juanita's Story   1

Three Factors for Academic Success   2

1. Know Why You're Here   2

2. Have a Sense of Personal Responsibility   3

3. Connect with Others   4

Your Personal Values and Motivation Can Help You Achieve Academic Success   6

Your Dreams Are Worth Pursuing   6

Your Values Drive Your Goals   7

Your Motivation Fuels Your Action   7

Set SMART Goals for Your Success   8

Your Goals Set the Bar for Achievement   8

Goal-Writing Tips   9

Write a Personal Mission Statement   10

Your Mission Statement Defines Your Purpose   10

■ Case Scenarios   12

■ Take It with You   13

■ Reference   13

CHAPTER 2   Time Management   15

Laura's Story   15

Now Is the Time to Develop an Effective Time-Management Strategy   16

Know Your Priorities   16

Using Tools Can Help You Manage Time   18

Calendars, Lists, and Workspaces   18

Routines Are Time-Management Tools   19

Looking Out for Time-Management Pitfalls   20

Avoid the "Black Holes" of Technology and Procrastination   20

Multitask in Moderation   22

Manage Your Energy   22

■ Case Scenarios   24

■ Take It with You   25

■ References   25

CHAPTER 3   Money Management   27

Evan's Story   27

Financial Literacy Is a Lifelong Lesson   28

Estimate Your College Costs   28

Create a Budget   29

Learn More about Your Finances   30

Set Financial Goals to Help Stay on Track   30

Having A Good Strategy Can Help You Manage Your Finances   32

Protect Yourself   32

Know the Advantages and Disadvantages of Using Credit Cards   32

Options for Paying for College   33

Scholarships   33

Grants   34

Student Loans   35

■ Case Scenarios   36

■ Take It with You   37

■ References   37

CHAPTER 4 Critical and Creative Thinking 39

Michael's Story 39

Critical-Thinking Skills Will Serve You Well 40

Creative Thinking Can Help You Develop New Ideas 42

Critical and Creative Thinking Can Help You Solve Problems 43

Step 1: Identify the Problem or Goal 44

Step 2: Generate Several Possible Solutions 44

Step 3: Critically Evaluate Each Solution 44

Step 4: Select a Solution and Put It into Action 45

Step 5: Evaluate the Solution 45

■ Case Scenarios 47

■ Take It with You 48

■ References 48

CHAPTER 5 Learning Style Preference 49

Juanita's, Michael's, Laura's, and Evan's Stories 49

Recognize the Different Types of Intelligence 50

Different Theories Provide Unique Insights 50

A Learning Style Inventory Can Help You Determine Your Learning Style Preference 52

VAK Survey 52

Your Classroom and Study Tactics Can Reflect Your Learning Style Preference 54

Visual Learners 55

Auditory Learners 55

Kinesthetic Learners 55

Choose a Study Strategy That Enhances Your Learning Style Preference 55

Use Your Learning Preferences to Explore Major and Career Options 57

■ Case Scenarios 59

■ Take It with You 60

■ References 60

CHAPTER 6 Listening and Note Taking 61

Laura's Story 61

Success In Class Begins with Preparation 62

Effective Listening Is Both Active And Critical 63

To Listen Critically Is to Listen Well 64

Taking Notes Is Part of the Listening Process 65

Knowing How Information Is Presented Can Improve Your Note Taking 66

Note-Taking Strategies: Pick What Works Best for You 68

■ Case Scenarios 71

■ Take It with You 72

■ Reference 72

CHAPTER 7 Reading and Note Taking 73

Evan's Story 73

Reading Is an Active Process 74

Successful Reading Begins with Preparation 74

Skimming and Scanning Can Be Useful Techniques 76

SQ3R Is a Useful Reading Strategy 76

Active Reading Also Means Critical Reading 77

Taking Good Notes Will Help You Become a Better Reader 78

Ebooks Are Coming! 79

Combining Your Class and Text Notes Will Give You the Whole Picture 79

■ Case Scenarios 81

■ Take It with You 82

■ Reference 82

CHAPTER 8 Studying and Test Taking 83

Four Students' Stories 83

Studying Is a Necessary Lifelong Habit 84

Using Memory Strategies Can Help You Remember and Learn More Deeply 85

Memorizing Is an Important Skill 85

Mnemonic Devices Can Help You Remember 85

Different Tests and Test Questions Require Using Different Strategies 88

Test Questions Will Vary, and So Should Your Answers 90

■ Case Scenarios 93

■ Take It with You 94

■ References 94

CHAPTER 9 Communication and Diversity 95

Michael's Story 95

Your Communication Needs to Fit a Diverse Audience 96

Value Diversity and Develop Cultural Competence 97

Recognize and Appreciate Diversity in Gender and Sexual Orientation 97

Racial, Ethnic, and Cultural Diversity Support Development of Cultural Competence 98

Generational Diversity Is More Prevalent Than Ever 98

Don't Overlook Socioeconomic Diversity 99

Adjusting Your Communication to Accommodate Diversity 99

Success In College Takes A Team Effort 100

Having Successful Group Projects 101

Conflict Will Happen, So Be Ready to Resolve It 102

Boundaries Provide Healthy Limits 102

Solving Problems Requires Following Procedures 103

■ Case Scenarios 105

■ Take It with You 106

■ References 106

CHAPTER 10 Information Literacy 107

Juanita's Story 107

Information Literacy Prepares You for Success 108

Know Different Ways to Find Appropriate Sources 109

Use Sources That Are Reliable, Credible, Current, and Accurate 111

Use Your Sources to Support Your Argument or Thesis 111

Evaluate Your Sources Carefully 112

Use Sources Ethically 113

Be Sure to Avoid Plagiarism 113

■ Case Studies 115

■ Take It with You 116

■ References 116

CHAPTER 11 Managing Stress 117

Evan's Story 117

College Has Stressors All Its Own 118

Knowing How You React To Stress Can Help You Manage It 119

You Can Manage Your Stress 119

Disarm the Negative Effects of Stress 121

Being Flexible Can Help Minimize Stress 123

Seek Help If Stress Becomes Overwhelming 123

Your Physical Health Is Important, Too 124

Nutrition Gives You Fuel 124

Exercise Gives You Energy and Relieves Stress 124

Sleep Recharges Your Batteries   124

Drugs and Alcohol Can Quickly Derail Your
Health and Life   124

Yes, We Do Need to Talk about Sex   125

Depression and Suicide Are Sad but Real
Occurrences in College   125

■ Case Scenarios   126

■ Take It with You   127

■ Reference   127

CHAPTER 12 Career Exploration   129

Evan and Michael's Story   129

Your Career Starts Here   130

Career Values and Goals Set the Course for
Your Journey   130

Different Careers Mean Different
Experiences   130

**There are Several Ways to Explore Your
Career   131**

Career Counselors Can Be Your Best
Supporters   132

Internships Give You and Your Employer a
Chance for a "Test Drive"   132

Networking Opens Doors for Your Career   133

Networking Is More than Exchanging Business
Cards   133

Networking Face to Face   134

Networking Online   135

**Your Resume Establishes Your Personal
Brand   136**

Your Resume Puts Your Life on Paper   136

■ Case Scenarios   139

■ Take It with You   140

■ References   140

Index   141

The College Experience Compact is different than any other text.

Digital is here. Students and instructors are engaging in more active learning and teaching. This requires a different kind of book. *The College Experience Compact* is developed specifically for hybrid and online environments, to address the needs and challenges of students as digital learners. It aligns with learning outcomes from both the Student Success CourseConnect online course and MyStudentSuccessLab, making it ideal as a print companion paired with one of these technologies for hybrid or online learning.

Organized by learning outcome, both Student Success CourseConnect and MyStudentSuccessLab promote student engagement and help students "Start strong, Finish stronger" by building skills for *ongoing personal and professional development*. Student Success CourseConnect (www.pearsonlearningsolutions.com/courseconnect) is one of many award-winning CourseConnect online courses designed by subject matter experts and credentialed instructional designers that supports a sequence of lessons, rich in content. MyStudentSuccessLab (www.mystudentsuccesslab.com) is an online solution with modules to support measurement using robust assessment with reporting capability, gradable activities, and professionalism topics.

Get only what you need. When students are taking (or instructors are teaching) 1 credit hour student success courses, it can be challenging to get through it all in the time available—and do so in an applied manner. There are a lot of "essentials' versions of books, but none offer the required "application" piece—until now.

The College Experience Compact provides students with the "unwritten rules" for college success by meeting them where they are, and helping to them develop a plan to handle the "when, when, and where" questions in any situation. When paired with Student Success CourseConnect or MyStudentSuccessLab as an online companion, it actively augments learning with activities, assessments, and extended thought-provoking exercises students need in order to understand how to apply concepts.

FROM THE AUTHORS

You have heard all of the clichés about college being a great time to discover who you are and who you want to be, while enjoying yourself during the process, but for many individuals—ourselves included—starting college was a time filled with nervousness and anxiety. Fortunately, we both had enrolled in colleges that understood first-year student issues and that helped us navigate the first few weeks and subsequent semesters with less fear, so that we became confident we could complete our degrees.

It is with that memory of what it was like to be a new student that this book has been written. It has *you* in mind. *You* are the one who got good grades in high school; now you have entered a new environment away from home and need to know what college is really like. Or maybe *you* are the one who didn't do as well as you wanted to in high school and are now committed to staying focused and getting your degree; you could use a little help honing your study skills. Or are *you* are the one who is returning to college after taking some time off to work and build a life? You could use some help meeting your college's expectations.

No matter where you're coming from and how excited you are about being in college for the first time—or again after some time away—things will be different, and any help you can get mastering the new "rules" of college will help you get a firm footing more quickly. This book has been written to help you do just that. Each chapter provides "just-in-time" information to help you master the key concepts of student success, and each feature within the chapters has been designed for real-world relevance. Think of this book as a resource manual for your first semester and beyond.

INTRODUCTION FOR FACULTY

As a professor, you know that student success doesn't just happen. Instead, it takes a combination of motivation, preparation, persistence, and relationships. You also know that no matter how prepared some students are for the academic challenges of college, they are not always ready for the cultural challenges, including understanding professors' expectations and navigating the financial issues that are part of the college experience. So much of what students are expected to know about being successful in college are "unwritten rules," and the rest of what they need to know is new information about how college works.

This book has been written to help you help your students by providing the clear, concise, and practical information that students need. Students are prompted to review important college documents such as the syllabus, consider how to make good choices and maintain their personal integrity, and analyze their own situations and apply the content to new ones. Specifically, students will learn what college expectations are and how to exceed them.

To that end, each lesson contains the following features with the focus on the "unwritten rules" or the "what, where, and when" for being successful in college.

"WHAT" WILL SUPPORT STUDENTS

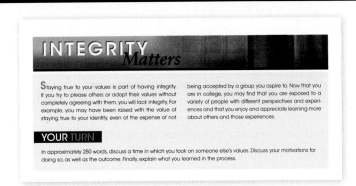

◀ **Integrity Matters**
Provides an opportunity to reflect on integrity issues that are both academic and personal, as integrity plays a major role in a student's life.

◀ **The Unwritten Rules**
Provides students with "insider" information about how college really works and makes information about expectations explicit.

"WHERE" CAN STUDENTS APPLY WHAT IS BEING LEARNED

It's in the Syllabus

Your professors' syllabi provide a number of clues that can help you develop SMART goals for academic success. For example, a syllabus for biology might list due dates and requirements for assignments, projects, and exams. You can establish some SMART goals that will help you succeed in this class, such as "Review a draft of my DNA project with my professor at least one week before it is due." Also think about these questions:

- What are the most important graded activities in each class?
- When are they due? What specific goals can you work towards to help you earn high scores on these graded activities?

◄ **It's in the Syllabus**

Reminds students to review one of the most important documents in college—the "contract" between their instructors and themselves—and asks them questions about the syllabus.

Meeting EXPECTATIONS

The college will expect that I . . .	To meet that expectation, I will . . .
Example: . . . read the assigned material before I get to class.	Example: . . . schedule time before every class to complete the required reading and review my notes.

◄ **Meeting Expectations**

Gives students the opportunity to reflect on the expectations of college and take on their personal responsibility to meet those expectations by creating action steps.

"WHEN" WILL STUDENTS RELATE TO THE MATERIAL

Take It with You

Action Item	Deadline	First Step
Review and update your Five "Whys?" for being in college (Activity 1) every term.		
Review and update your Who's in Your Circle? diagram (Activity 2) twice a year.		
Review and update your Three S.M.A.R.T Goals for the Semester (Activity 3) every term.		
Write your Personal Mission Statement (Activity 4).		

◄ **Take It with You**

Allows students to create an action plan for taking the strategies they have learned and incorporating it into their own lives, by choosing a goal, timeframe, and action step.

CASE SCENARIOS

1. In Jennifer's literature class, she is reading Tim O'Brien's novel *The Things They Carried*. Although she understands that the novel is about the Vietnam War, she doesn't know why she has to read a book that contains so much profanity and graphic images of death. Jennifer has made an appointment to speak to her professor about the assignment, because she wants to get out of reading a book that is so depressing and disturbing. She is prepared to suggest that she read and write a paper on a Shakespearean play instead—a paper that she did in high school and got an A on.

Use the following scale to rate the decision that has been made (1 = Poor Decision, 5 = Excellent Decision). Be prepared to explain your answer.

Poor Decision ◄——(1)——(2)——(3)——(4)——(5)—► Excellent Decision

2. Jai-Ling is taking a biology class. One of her assignments is to create a group presentation on an assigned topic. Her group's topic is the theory of evolution, a theory that Jai-Ling finds fascinating, even though all she knows about it is what little she learned in high school. When Jai-Ling meets with her group to begin work on the presentation, two group members express deep concern about being asked to study something that they don't believe in. They refuse to help with the project, even though they know their lack of participation will lower the whole group's grade. Jai-Ling tells these group members that they are being immature and ridiculous, because one of the purposes of being in college is to be challenged in one's thinking. She goes straight to the professor to complain and to ask to be assigned to a new group.

◄ **Case Scenarios**

Provides scenarios about real-life decisions on issues students' face, and to evaluate the choices they make and discuss how they arrived at their judgments.

INTRODUCTION FOR STUDENTS

You made it! You have taken the first steps toward getting a college education, and for that, you should feel a sense of accomplishment. It's no easy task to apply for admission, enroll in classes, and find your way around campus, but you have obviously completed those steps successfully. Getting your course supplies, such as textbooks and notebooks, is also a feat worth congratulating. Now, it's time to take a moment and think about why you are here and what you hope to achieve.

W. Edwards Deming, professor and industrial consultant, once said, "It's not enough to do your best. You must know what to do and then do your best." Obviously, your commitment to take the first step into college shows that you have the desire to do your best. Now you just need the tools to help you know what to do so that you can do your best in college, in your career, and in your life.

The student case studies allow you to consider what life will be like for you now that you are in college. These scenarios are about real-life decisions on issues students face, and how to evaluate the choices they make and discuss how they arrived at their judgments. They will help you see how others experience college for the first time and help you see how you can meet the challenges you will surely face as a new student.

Features—such as Meeting Expectations, The Unwritten Rules, and the updated Take It with You—have been designed to empower you. Not only do they provide you with the "insider secrets" of success, but they also give you the opportunity to create action steps to meet the new expectations of college.

Another feature, Integrity Matters, will remind you of one of the core values of higher education: integrity, or doing what is right even if no one is watching. This feature provides opportunities to explore acting with integrity—a good habit to acquire during college. The feature called It's in the Syllabus will help to demystify that handout you get from each of your professors. You will be able to transform the syllabus from a piece of paper into a tool that helps you succeed.

This entire book has been written with your best interests in mind. May it serve you well as you take the first steps toward your future!

MyStudentSuccessLab is an online solution designed to help students acquire the skills they need to succeed for ongoing personal and professional development. They will have access to peer-led video interviews and develop core skills through interactive practice exercises and activities that provide academic, life, and professionalism skills that will transfer to ANY course.

How can "skills" be measured – and what can you do with the data?

Measurement Matters – and is ongoing in nature. No one is ever an "expert" in 'soft skills' – something students learn once and never think about again. They take these skills with them for life.

Learning Path Diagnostic

- For the course, 65 Pre-Course questions (Levels I & II Bloom's) and 65 Post-Course questions (Levels III & IV Bloom's) that link to key learning objectives in each topic.

- For each topic, 20 Pre-Test questions (Levels I & II Bloom's) and 20 Post-Test questions (Levels III & IV Bloom's) that link to all learning objectives in the topic.

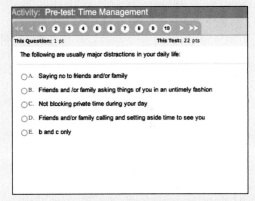

What gets your attention?

It's about engagement. Everyone likes videos.
Good videos, conveniently organized by topic.

FinishStrong247 YouTube channel

- Best of 'how to' for use as a practical reference
  (i.e. — manage your priorities using a smart phone)

- Save time finding good video.

- All videos have been approved by members of our student advisory board and peer reviewed.

How can everyone get trained?

We all want a 'shortcut to implementation.'
Instructors want to save time on course prep.
Students want to know how to register, log in, and know 'what's due, and when.'
We can make it easy.

Implementation Guide

- Organized by topic, provides time on task, grading rubrics, suggestions for video use, and more.

- Additional videos and user guides, registration and log in guides, and technical support for instructors and students at www.mystudentsuccesslab.com

MyStudentSuccessLab Feature set:

Learning Path provides:
- 65 Pre-Course (Levels I & II Bloom's) and 65 Post-Course (Levels III & IV Bloom's)
- 20 Pre-Test (Levels I & II Bloom's) and 20 Post-Test (Levels III & IV Bloom's)
- Overview (i.e. – Learning Outcomes)
- Student Video Interviews (with Reflection questions)
- Practices and Activities Tied to Learning Path
- FinishStronger247 YouTube channel with student-vetted supporting videos

Student Inventories:
1. **Golden Personality**—Similar to Meyers Briggs—it offers a personality assessment and robust reporting for students to get actionable insights on personal style. www. talentlens.com/en/employee-assessments/golden.php

2. **ACES (Academic Competence Evaluation Scales)**—Strength inventory that identifies and screens students to help educators prioritize skills and provides an overview of how students see themselves as learners. Identifies at-risk students. www.pearsonassessments.com/HAIWEB/Cultures/en-us/ Productdetail.htm?Pid=015-8005-805

3. **(Watson-Glaser) Thinking Styles**—Helps students understand their thought process and how they tend to approach situations. Shows how you make decisions. www.thinkwatson.com/mythinkingstyles

Student Resources:
Pearson Students Facebook page, FinishStrong247 YouTube channel, MySearchLab, Online Dictionary, Plagiarism Guide, Student Planner, MyProfessionalismKit resources including video cases. GPA, Savings, Budgeting, and Retirement Calculators.

Instructor Resources:
Instructor Implementation Guide supports course prep with Overview, Time on Task, Grading rubric, etc.

MyStudentSuccessLab Topic List:

A First Step: Goal Setting	Memory and Studying
Communication	Problem Solving
Critical Thinking	Reading and Annotating
Financial Literacy	Stress Management
Information Literacy	Teamwork
Interviewing	Test Taking
Job Search Strategies	Time Management
Learning Preferences	Workplace Communication (formerly 'Professionalism')
Listening and Taking Notes in Class	Workplace Etiquette
Majors/Careers and Resumes	

MyLabsPlus Available upon request for MyStudentSuccessLab

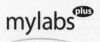

MyLabsPlus service is a dynamic online teaching and learning environment designed to support online instruction programs with rich, engaging customized content. With powerful administrator tools and dedicated support, MyLabsPlus is designed to support growing online instruction programs with an advanced suite of management tools. Working in conjunction with MyLabs and Mastering content and technology, schools can quickly and easily integrate MyLabsPlus into their curriculum.

Student Success CourseConnect

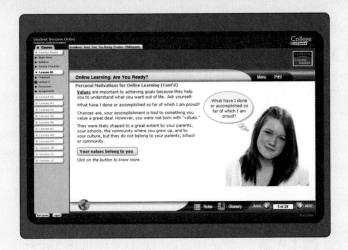 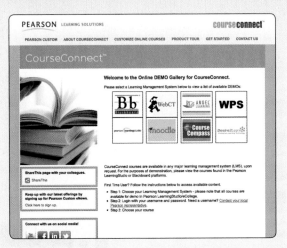

Student Success CourseConnect (http://www.pearsonlearningsolutions.com/courseconnect) is one of many award-winning CourseConnect customizable online courses designed by subject matter experts and credentialed instructional designers, and helps students 'Start strong, Finish stronger' by building skills for ongoing personal and professional development.

Topic-based interactive modules follow a consistent learning path, from Introduction, to Presentation, to Activity, then Review. Student Success CourseConnect is available in your school's learning management system (LMS) and includes relevant video, audio, and activities. Syllabi, discussion forum topics and questions, assignments, and quizzes are easily accessible and it accommodates various term lengths as well as self-paced study.

Course Outline (i.e. 'Lesson Plans')

1. Goal setting, Values, and Motivation
2. Time Management
3. Financial Literacy
4. Creative Thinking, Critical Thinking, and Problem Solving
5. Learning Preferences
6. Listening and Note-Taking in Class
7. Reading and Annotating
8. Studying, Memory, and Test-Taking
9. Communicating and Teamwork
10. Information Literacy
11. Staying Balanced: Stress Management
12. Career Exploration

"What makes my CourseConnect course so successful is all the engagement that is built-in for students. My students really benefit from the videos, and all the interactivity that goes along with the classes that I've designed for them."

—Kelly Kirk, Director of Distance Education, Randolph Community College

"It's truly great that Pearson is invested in using the latest technologies to reach me in ways beside the traditional educational model. This innovative approach is one of the best ways to facilitate the education of students of my generation."

—Zach Gonzales, Student, University of Denver

Resources for Online Learning or Hybrid

PART I	BEFORE CLASS	
Chapter 1	Becoming an Online Learner	1
Chapter 2	Know Thyself: Self-Discovery for the Online Learner	9
Chapter 3	Motivation and Goal Setting: Overcoming Obstacles	15
Chapter 4	The Commitments of an Online Student: Managing Your Priorities	23
PART II	ABOUT CLASS	
Chapter 5	The Online Classroom and Community	31
Chapter 6	Navigating Learning Management Systems	37
Chapter 7	The Hybrid Balance	49
PART III	IN CLASS	
Chapter 8	Communicating Online: Who, What, When, How, and Why	55
Chapter 9	Working in the Online Classroom	63
Chapter 10	Thinking and Researching Online	
Chapter 11	Strategies for Successful Online Learning	
Chapter 12	The Evolution of Learning	
PART IV	TOOLS AND WORKSPACE	
Chapter 13	Computer Concerns	
Chapter 14	E-Books: The Evolution of the Textbook	
Chapter 15	Creating the Ideal Personalized Study Environment	
PART V	EMPOWER YOU	
Chapter 16	Preparing for the First Day of Class	
Chapter 17	Maintaining Your Online Success	
Appendix A	Financing Your Education	
Appendix B	Understanding the Importance of Accreditation	

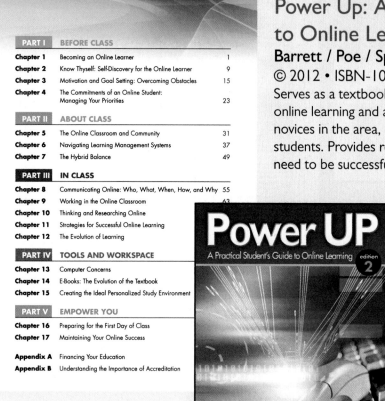

Power Up: A Practical Student's Guide to Online Learning, 2/e

Barrett / Poe / Spagnola-Doyle

© 2012 • ISBN-10: 0132788195 • ISBN-13: 9780132788199

Serves as a textbook for students of all backgrounds who are new to online learning and as a reference book for instructors who are also novices in the area, or who need insight into the perspective of such students. Provides readers with the knowledge and practice they need to be successful online learners.

"We have used this excellent text with all cohorts of the last two years, as the text is an integral part of the first course in our graduate online program. Students love that it's user-friendly and practical. Instructors see this text as a powerful learning tool that is concise yet is able to be comprehensive in its coverage of critical skills and knowledge that support online student success."

—Dr. William Prado
Associate Professor & Director,
Business Program, Green Mountain College

Introducing CourseSmart, The world's largest online marketplace for digital texts and course materials.

A Smarter Way for Students

CourseSmart is convenient. Students have instant access to exactly the materials their instructor assigns.

CourseSmart offers choice. With CourseSmart, students have a high-quality alternative to the print textbook.

CourseSmart saves money. CourseSmart digital solutions can be purchased for up to 50% less than traditional print textbooks.

CourseSmart offers education value. Students receive the same content offered in the print textbook enhanced by the search, note-taking, and printing tools of a web application.

CourseSmart is the Smarter Way

To learn for yourself, visit
www.coursesmart.com

Resources

Online Instructor's Manual — This manual is intended to give instructors a framework or blueprint of ideas and suggestions that may assist them in providing their students with activities, journal writing, thought-provoking situations, and group activities.

Online PowerPoint Presentation — A comprehensive set of PowerPoint slides that can be used by instructors for class presentations and also by students for lecture preview or review. The PowerPoint Presentation includes bullet point slides with overview information for each chapter. These slides help students understand and review concepts within each chapter.

Assessment via MyStudentSuccessLab — It is an online solution—*and powerful assessment tool*—designed to help students build the skills they need to succeed for ongoing personal and professional development at www.mystudentsuccesslab.com

Create tests using a secure testing engine within MyStudentSuccessLab (similar to Pearson MyTest) to print or deliver online. The high quality and volume of test questions allows for data comparison and measurement, which is highly sought after and frequently required from institutions.

- Quickly create a test within MyStudentSuccessLab for use online or to save to Word or PDF format and print
- Draws from a rich library of question test banks that complement course learning outcomes
- Like the option in former test managers (MyTest and TestGen), test questions in MyStudentSuccessLab are organized by learning outcome
- On National average, Student Success materials are customized by 78% of instructors—in both sequence and depth of materials, so organizing by learning outcomes (as opposed to 'chapter') saves customers' time
- Questions that test specific learning outcomes in a text chapter are easy to find by using the ACTIVITIES/ASSESSMENTS MANAGER in MyStudentSuccessLab
- MyStudentSuccessLab allows for personalization with the ability to edit individual questions or entire tests to accommodate specific teaching needs
- Because MyStudentSuccessLab is written to learning outcomes, this technology has breadth across any course where 'soft skills' are being addressed

LASSI — The LASSI is a 10-scale, 80-item assessment of students' awareness about and use of learning and study strategies. Addressing skill, will, and self-regulation, the focus is on both covert and overt thoughts, behaviors, attitudes and beliefs that relate to successful learning and that can be altered through educational interventions.

Noel Levitz/RMS — This retention tool measures Academic Motivation, General Coping Ability, Receptivity to Support Services, PLUS Social Motivation. It helps identify at-risk students, the areas with which they struggle, and their receptiveness to support.

Premier Annual Planner — This specially designed, annual 4-color collegiate planner includes an academic planning/resources section, monthly planning section (2 pages/month), and weekly planning section (48 weeks; July start date). The Premier Annual Planner facilitates short-term as well as long-term planning. This text is spiral bound and convenient to carry with a 6 x 9 inch trim size.

Custom Publishing

As the industry leader in custom publishing, we are committed to meeting your instructional needs by offering flexible and creative choices for course materials that will maximize learning and engagement of students.

The Pearson Custom Library

Using our online book-building system, www.pearsoncustomlibrary.com, create a custom book by selecting content from our course-specific collections that consist of chapters from Pearson Student Success and Career Development titles and carefully selected, copyright cleared, third-party content, and pedagogy.
www.pearsonlearningsolutions.com/custom-library/pearson-custom-student-success-and-career-development

Custom Publications

In partnership with your Custom Field Editor, modify, adapt, and combine existing Pearson books by choosing content from across the curriculum and organize it around your learning outcomes. As an alternative, work with them to develop your original material and create a textbook that meets your course goals.
www.pearsonlearningsolutions.com/custom-publications

Custom Technology Solutions

Work with Pearson's trained professionals, in a truly consultative process, to create engaging learning solutions. From interactive learning tools to eTexts, to custom websites and portals, we'll help you simplify your life as an instructor.
www.pearsonlearningsolutions.com/higher-education/customizable-technology-resources.php

Online Education

Offers online course content for online learning classes, hybrid courses, and enhances the traditional classroom. Our award-winning product CourseConnect includes a fully developed syllabus, media-rich lecture presentations, audio lectures, a wide variety of assessments, discussion board questions, and a strong instructor resource package.
www.pearsonlearningsolutions.com/higher-education/customizable-online-courseware.php

For more information on how Pearson Custom Student Success can work for you, please visit **www.pearsonlearningsolutions.com** or call 800-777-6872

1 Your Mission Statement and Goals

Juanita called her mother for the second time in two hours. She had just created her schedule and visited with her advisor about earning a degree in nursing. She sent a text to her mother that said "Call me," and her mother called immediately.

"Do you think I can do this?" Juanita asked.

"Juanita," her mother said with softness and fatigue in her voice, "you always overthink these things. I know you like to be prepared, but things will be different in college. It's not high school."

The classes Juanita had registered for seemed different from the ones she had taken in high school.

"Yeah," Juanita replied, "but I didn't have to make a life decision in high school. It made me nervous when my advisor asked me to choose a degree plan and write out goals for completing my degree."

"You did choose electrical engineering, just like we talked about, right?" her mother asked.

"Well, I wanted to talk to you about that," Juanita said. "I saw a flyer about careers in the health field. I could make a really good salary as a nurse right after I graduate."

"But you don't like working with people who are sick, Juanita," her mother replied. "When you were younger, you were always building things in the backyard."

Juanita knew her mother wanted her to become an engineer because Juanita's mother's father had been one. Juanita's family also wanted her to "use her brain" in a prestigious field. But Juanita thought nursing would be a better fit for her, especially because her father's sister was a nurse and loved her job. Juanita decided to keep her degree plan in nursing and to tell her mother about her choice later.

Like Juanita, you'll face some important decisions in college that will require you to have a clear sense of why you're in college and what you're trying to accomplish. To help you get on the right track, this chapter will help you do the following:

- Incorporate three factors for academic success into your life.
- Analyze the relationship among values, motivation, and goals for academic success.
- Use the characteristics of SMART goals in your goal setting.
- Write your mission statement.

LEARNING OUTCOME

Create long- and short-term goals that align with your personal mission statement.

THREE FACTORS FOR ACADEMIC SUCCESS

Congratulations, you've made it to college! Your journey to this point may not have been easy, but you're here and you're ready to succeed. We wrote this book because we want to help you succeed.

Do you realize that only about 6% of the entire world's population has earned a college degree? You have the opportunity to earn a distinction that relatively few people on this planet will experience, and you deserve a lot of credit for pursuing this noble achievement.

What will it take for you to be successful in college? This book is filled with ideas, suggestions, and strategies to help you succeed. In this chapter, we provided the foundational information you will need to start strong and finish stronger. In this section, however, we've narrowed our list of ingredients for success to three of the most important elements: know why you're here; have a sense of personal responsibility; and connect with others.

1. Know Why You're Here

A popular problem-solving approach in some organizational circles is called *root cause analysis*. It describes the effort to uncover the root cause, or primary reason, for a particular outcome or circumstance.

One technique for uncovering the root cause of something is to ask "Why?" five times, as shown in the following example:

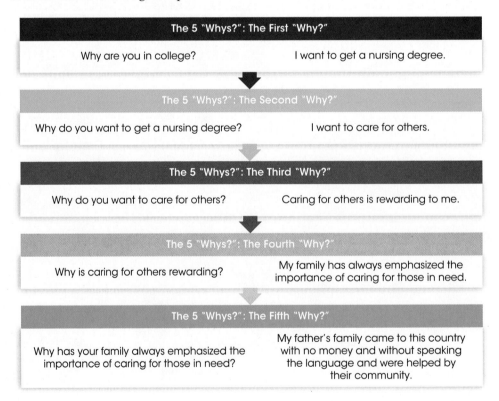

The 5 "Whys?": The First "Why?"	
Why are you in college?	I want to get a nursing degree.

The 5 "Whys?": The Second "Why?"	
Why do you want to get a nursing degree?	I want to care for others.

The 5 "Whys?": The Third "Why?"	
Why do you want to care for others?	Caring for others is rewarding to me.

The 5 "Whys?": The Fourth "Why?"	
Why is caring for others rewarding?	My family has always emphasized the importance of caring for those in need.

The 5 "Whys?": The Fifth "Why?"	
Why has your family always emphasized the importance of caring for those in need?	My father's family came to this country with no money and without speaking the language and were helped by their community.

Let's start with a simple first question—"Why are you in college?"—and then ask four more "Whys?" after that. For example, if your answer to "Why are you in college" is "I want to get a nursing degree," then the next question is "Why do you want to get a nursing degree?" If your answer to that question is "I want to care for others," then ask yourself another "Why?"

As you proceed with asking yourself five "Whys?" you'll get deeper and deeper into your true motivations for pursuing a college degree. You'll also have a much clearer understanding of yourself and why you are in college.

Take a moment to complete Activity 1, The Five "Whys?"

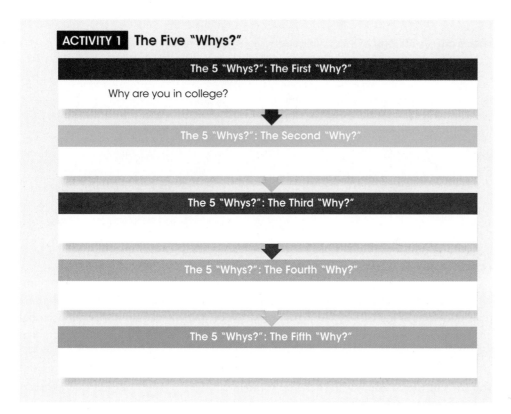

ACTIVITY 1 **The Five "Whys?"**

The 5 "Whys?": The First "Why?"

Why are you in college?

The 5 "Whys?": The Second "Why?"

The 5 "Whys?": The Third "Why?"

The 5 "Whys?": The Fourth "Why?"

The 5 "Whys?": The Fifth "Why?"

2. Have a Sense of Personal Responsibility

Exhibit 1 illustrates some of the differences and similarities among going to high school, working at a full-time job, and attending college. As you read down through the column labeled "College" in Exhibit 1, you'll notice that a pattern emerges: Compared to going to high school or working full time, attending college involves a dramatic increase in the amount of personal responsibility an individual must handle. High school teachers and job supervisors provide clear guidance, both about expectations and how to achieve them. In college, however, students are responsible for understanding the expectations for academic and career success based on information from the college catalog, course syllabi, and class assignments, and must develop strategies for meeting those expectations.

During your high school or work experience, you probably wished at times that you had more freedom to make your own decisions and to pursue your own interests. As you step into college, your wishes will indeed come true. The range of opportunities and alternatives that lie before you is so broad and diverse that you'll find yourself making important decisions every day.

Knowing why you are in college will help you figure out where you want to go.

EXHIBIT 1   Differences among High School, Full-Time Work, and College

High School	Full-Time Work	College
Attendance is mandatory to meet requirements.	Attendance is mandatory to stay employed.	Attendance may not be mandatory to meet requirements.
At least six continuous hours are spent in class each day.	At least eight continuous hours are spent at work each day.	Different amounts of time are spent in class and between classes each day.
Moderate to no outside work is necessary to complete requirements.	Moderate to no overtime work is necessary to complete job duties.	Substantial amount of outside work is necessary to complete assignments and be successful.
Teachers go over material and expect students to remember facts and information.	Employers provide basic information and expect employees to use it to complete their jobs effectively.	Professors provide concepts and theories and expect students to evaluate ideas, synthesize the ideas with other concepts they have learned, and develop new ideas.

Having this level of personal responsibility is exciting, but it can also be overwhelming at times. You may even find yourself suffering significant consequences for making poor decisions along the way. To avoid these problems, you should develop a personal approach that you can use as you step into an experience that offers so much personal responsibility and autonomy.

Complete the Meeting Expectations exercise by choosing a college expectation that you will encounter and writing an action statement for how you will meet that expectation through personal responsibility.

3. Connect with Others

Even the most dedicated student can't do it all alone. In fact, behind every successful college graduate is a good support system, usually comprised of family, friends, and community members.

It's no secret that succeeding in college will take more than just studying hard. You'll need to surround yourself with people who encourage you to do your best. At times, you'll need others for academic, emotional, and even financial support. Recognizing

Meeting EXPECTATIONS

The college will expect that I ...	To meet that expectation, I will ...
Example: . . . *read the assigned material before I get to class.*	Example: . . . *schedule time before every class to complete the required reading and review my notes.*
_____	_____
_____	_____
_____	_____

who in your circle of friends, family, and contacts will be the best resources is part of the process of creating the support system that will inevitably be part of your college success.

Professors

Perhaps no one will be more important to your college success and possible future career success than your professors. They don't just provide you with access to the content and challenge you to think critically about the subject matter. They can also be mentors and resources as you complete your degree and begin your career. One way to start out on the right path to good relationships with your professors is to greet them with a smile and a "Hello" when you see them in and out of class.

Advisors, Counselors, and Administrators

In addition to professors, some of the most important relationships that you will create during college will be with people whose sole job is to help you succeed. Counselors and advisors will be key people in your academic career, so be sure to take the time to get to know them. College administrators also play an important role.

Your advisor may be the first person you encounter at college. Your advisor will explain what courses you should take, how many credit hours you should take a semester, and how to plan your remaining semesters. You may be lucky enough to have the same advisor throughout your college career. In that case, having regular contact with your advisor will help keep the lines of communication open. If you have a different advisor each semester, you may want to find one person who can act as a regular advisor.

Family

Whether you live with your parents, are a parent yourself, or fall somewhere in between, your family is an important part of who you are and what you will become. Your family has influenced your values and beliefs, and they may be part of the reason you've enrolled in college. For many students, being able to stay in college and be successful depends on having the support of their families. If your family will be an important part of your life as you pursue a degree, then you will need to consider how they will support you and what you need to communicate to them about what to expect when you have to spend more time studying and taking classes than enjoying your relationships with them.

Friends

Another important part of your support system is your friends. While you may not be able to determine how your family members will influence your college experience, you will have some control over how your friends will influence that experience. If you have friends who have attended or are attending college, you'll have a great opportunity to connect with them on that common pursuit. Even if you and your friends don't attend the same college, you can develop a support system with them, since you will all be having similar experiences. You can share advice and study strategies, and you can lean on each other when you feel stressed. Knowing that a friend is having a similar experience can give you the motivation to continue working hard.

Roommates

If you choose to live in a dorm or apartment during your college career, you'll discover that your roommates can be either very positive or, unfortunately, very negative influences on your life. Roommates who share your goals and values and are as committed as you to being successful in college can provide a strong support system. They can offer encouragement when you're feeling discouraged and companionship when you're feeling lonely. You can provide the same support to them. It will be important for you to have study habits and personal strategies of your own, but at times, you'll benefit greatly from experiencing college life with roommates, with whom you can share meals, social activities, and household chores.

Complete Activity 2, Who's in Your Circle? by adding the people from the groups discussed in the previous sections in the outer circles.

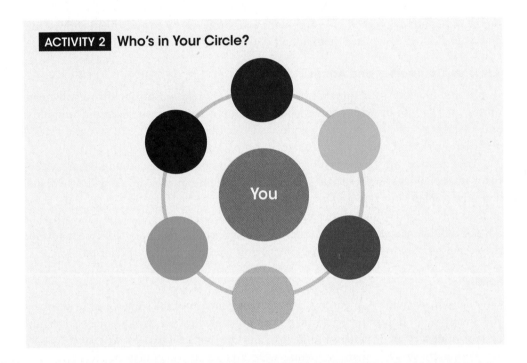

ACTIVITY 2 Who's in Your Circle?

You

YOUR PERSONAL VALUES AND MOTIVATION CAN HELP YOU ACHIEVE ACADEMIC SUCCESS

Your Dreams Are Worth Pursuing

As you consider your goals, also think about your dreams. Dreams are the big ideas and bold achievements that you sometimes imagine and secretly hope for. What do you want to do or achieve that you have not written down because you feel it is too far-fetched?

There are many stories of people who ignored their dreams and took jobs that provided financial security and prestige, only to discover that their lives were not fulfilled because they regretted giving up on their dreams. There are also many exciting stories about people who never forgot their dreams and who achieved them eventually through hard work and determination.

Why don't more people follow their dreams? First, some people don't know what their dreams are. Their day-to-day lives take up so much of their time, attention, and energy that they don't take time to consider their dreams. Second, some people are scared. Pursuing your dreams is a risky proposition. There's always the chance that circumstances or events will bring disappointment and failure in this pursuit. Third, some people need to make the "safe" choice first before they can feel confident about pursuing their dreams.

You may not be able to fulfill your dreams in the immediate future, but don't lose sight of them.

INTEGRITY *Matters*

Staying true to your values is part of having integrity. If you try to please others or adopt their values without completely agreeing with them, you will lack integrity. For example, you may have been raised with the value of staying true to your identity, even at the expense of not being accepted by a group you aspire to. Now that you are in college, you may find that you are exposed to a variety of people with different perspectives and experiences and that you enjoy and appreciate learning more about others and those experiences.

YOUR TURN

In approximately 250 words, discuss a time in which you took on someone else's values. Discuss your motivations for doing so, as well as the outcome. Finally, explain what you learned in the process.

Your Values Drive Your Goals

Your life story will reflect your system of values. Values can be inherited from your parents, or they can be based on what your culture, religion, or ethnicity regard as important. Values can also be formed from both positive and negative experiences.

For example, one of your values may be honesty, which means that you try to be truthful and straightforward and you expect others to be honest with you. You may also value hard work, which means that you strive to do your best in your life. If a friend has treated you with compassion, you may value sensitivity to others. On the other hand, if you have been discriminated against in the past, you may now value open-mindedness in others.

The importance of knowing and understanding your values is that having this knowledge can help you set realistic goals. If you value a satisfying career, for instance, you will set goals that support that value. You will probably investigate fields and careers that are challenging and interesting. If you value a stable financial future, you will set goals that allow you to earn enough money to provide for your needs and wants. If you value your family, you will make spending time with them a priority. Your values should be a true reflection of who you are and what you believe.

Your Motivation Fuels Your Action

Motivation is the driving force behind action. You won't act unless you are motivated to do so. Your motivation determines whether you will put forth the time, thought, and effort to achieve your goals and dreams.

When was the last time you felt really motivated to do something? Maybe you just watched an inspirational movie, got a raise at work, or received some words of encouragement from a friend or relative. Or perhaps an event or circumstance—such as running into an old friend whose life has turned in a bad direction—has helped you realize that you need to take action to avoid a similar event or circumstance in your life. Regardless of the source of your motivation, you know that when you feel motivated, you are compelled to take action in pursuit of your dreams.

Of course, there will be times in your academic career when you will feel overwhelmed by the responsibilities you have and perhaps unsure of your ability to handle them all. When you feel weighed down by all that you have to accomplish during a particular day or week, try to calm down. If you can, talk with a friend, instructor, or

THE UNWRITTEN RULES
Of Motivation, Goals, and Mission Statements

- **Internal motivation is the key to success.** If most of your reasons for attending college are based on what others have told you or if your motivations for succeeding in college are driven mostly by others' expectations, you'll need to dig deeper to discover the reasons *you* want to succeed. Find your internal motivation for college success, even if it takes a while to discover it.

- **Everyone is motivated by something.** Your professors have their own motivations and goals, which you can use to help you understand them better, but they may not give you these details in writing or even tell you what they are. As you get to know your professors in class, during office hours, or as faculty advisors to student clubs and organizations, ask questions and listen for clues to help you understand what motivates them.

- **Relationships and motivations go hand in hand.** If you can uncover and understand what motivates someone and what he or she is trying to accomplish in life, you'll be better equipped to have a good personal and working relationship with that person. A great way to have good relationships is to understand people and know what drives them.

counselor and explain your frustration and stress. To stay motivated and to resist the temptation to give up, remind yourself of why you are doing what you are doing.

It might be helpful to revisit Activity 1, The Five Whys?" which you completed earlier in the chapter. Your answers to the fourth and fifth questions may lead you to or remind you of why you are in college, why you want to succeed, and what you want to accomplish.

SET SMART GOALS FOR YOUR SUCCESS

Your Goals Set the Bar for Achievement

To build on your mission statement—and to fulfill that mission in the process—you'll need to set goals that you can achieve. A *goal* is something that you work toward. It may be to learn how to cook macaroni and cheese, to quit a bad habit, or to write a novel.

Whatever your goals, they should be reasonable and attainable in the time frame that you have assigned. For instance, if you want to lose 10 pounds in one week, you may need to rethink the time frame in which you can achieve your goal. A more reasonable goal would be to lose 10 pounds in four months. Reasonable goals are more likely to be met.

As you begin to think about your goals, consider dividing them into long-term goals and short-term goals. Certainly, one of your long-term goals is to earn a degree. Achieving this goal may take a year or more, depending

The only way to know if are successful is to have a goal to aim for.

on how many degree requirements you need to complete or how many other responsibilities you may have.

When you write out your goals, use the acronym SMART. Your goals should be specific, measurable, attainable, realistic, and time specific, as outlined in Exhibit 2. Following are three goals that a college student might set. Let's apply the SMART approach to improve each one:

"Get good grades in college." This is a noble goal, certainly, but it's neither measurable nor time specific. "Achieve a 3.4 GPA at the end of my first term" specifies how you'll measure the goal (GPA) and by when (at the end of your first term).

"Earn extra money to pay for college." A lot of students will have this kind of goal for their college experience, but the goal needs to be measurable and time specific. "Generate an extra $2,000 in income before the beginning of fall semester" establishes a specific amount and a timeline.

> ### EXHIBIT **2** SMART Goals
>
> **Specific**—A goal should describe one specific outcome, such as losing 12 pounds.
>
> **Measurable**—A goal should describe an outcome that is observable and measurable. For example, weight loss can be measured on a scale.
>
> **Attainable**—A goal can be challenging but also something that you believe you can achieve or attain in the time frame that you give it.
>
> **Realistic**—Losing 12 pounds in two weeks is probably unrealistic and even unhealthy, but losing 12 pounds in twelve weeks is more realistic.
>
> **Time specific**—A goal should specify the time frame for achievement, so that you can gauge your progress and success. If your goal is simply to lose 12 pounds but you don't specify a time period, you won't know whether you're on track or what your deadline is for achieving it. Establishing a measurable deadline will allow you to celebrate your accomplishment on that day or time!

"Build a network of people who can help me get a job." Business students, in particular, are often told about the importance of networking, but expressing that activity as a goal can be challenging. It might be helpful to break the activity into some specific action items and to use them to establish goals. For example, a first-year student could start networking successfully by setting the following goal: "Personally meet and obtain business cards from at least 10 business or community leaders by the end of this academic year."

Goal-Writing Tips

Here are a few other tips for writing effective goals:

- *Write down your goals.* No matter what you want to achieve, be sure to write down all your goals. Then review them every few months to assess your progress.
- *Break larger goals into smaller goals that will lead to fulfillment.* Smaller goals are easier to achieve and can build quickly into a larger, long-term goal.
- *Review your goals regularly and make changes as necessary.* Circumstances and events beyond your control may require you to adjust your goals from time to

Write down specific, measurable goals and mark them off as you meet them.

It's in the SYLLABUS

Your professors' syllabi provide a number of clues that can help you develop SMART goals for academic success. For example, a syllabus for biology might list due dates and requirements for assignments, projects, and exams. You can establish some SMART goals that will help you succeed in this class, such as "Review a draft of my DNA project with my professor at least one week before it is due." Also think about these questions:

- What are the most important graded activities in each class?
- When are they due? What specific goals can you work towards to help you earn high scores on these graded activities?

time. Or you may set goals early on that change over time, as you discover new things about yourself or learn about new career and personal opportunities.

- *Reach out to others who care about you to help you achieve your goals.* Communicate your goals to your coworkers, family members, and friends. Enlist them to help you meet your goals, especially if you need to schedule time to study, to complete assignments, and so on. Managing your time will be much easier if your priorities and goals are concrete, realistic, and communicated to those around you.
- *Identify habits and challenges that may interfere with achieving your goals.* As you work toward your goals, make an effort to eliminate anything that keeps you from focusing on them. If you don't think you have time to accomplish two short-term goals during the week, examine where you have been spending your time and eliminate the activities that don't contribute to your goals. If you watch seven hours of television a week and aren't achieving the desired short-term goal of relaxing or becoming more informed, then spend that time doing something that contributes to your goal.

Complete Activity 3, Three SMART Goals for the Semester, by identifying three goals you would like to meet this term. Be sure to follow the guidelines for setting SMART goals.

ACTIVITY 3 Three SMART Goals for the Semester	
Goals	
SMART Goal 1	
SMART Goal 2	
SMART Goal 3	

WRITE A PERSONAL MISSION STATEMENT

Your Mission Statement Defines Your Purpose

A *mission statement* is a statement of purpose. Most companies and other organizations develop a mission statement to define a purpose and to answer crucial questions such as "Why do we exist?" and "What do we want to achieve?"

Your personal mission statement should explain your purpose in life from a very broad perspective. It should describe how your values, motivations, and goals will create your life's mission. Once you've identified your values, motivations, and goals, your next step is to craft your mission statement, which will establish your purpose. As you meet your goals and learn new things, your purpose will likely change and your mission statement will need to be revised.

The following is an example of a personal mission statement that you can use as a model for writing your own:

Sample Personal Mission Statement

As a nurse and educator, my life's mission is to work in a large research hospital and teach future nurses. By supporting my values of compassion, education, and job security, I work toward my life's mission by completing my nursing degree, working in different hospital environments, and training other nurses.

Practice writing your own mission statement in Activity 4, My Mission Statement, by filling in the blanks with the information that is suggested. Use your work in this activity to revise and refine your mission statement as you begin to meet your goals.

ACTIVITY 4 **My Mission Statement**

My Mission Statement

As a _____(dream/career/job/role), my life's

mission is to _____ (long-term goal). By supporting

my values of _____, _____, and _____,

I work toward my life's mission by _____, _____,

and _____ (short-term goals).

Because your mission statement describes your purpose in life, it's a very personalized statement—one that captures your dreams, values, and goals. Your mission statement should serve as a guidepost that you review on a regular basis to help you evaluate your life and determine whether the activities you are investing in on a daily basis are contributing to or hindering achievement of your purpose in life.

Take some time to write your personal mission statement, and share it with people in your life who are trustworthy and supportive of your success. Invite their input and make changes as needed, and then keep the final version somewhere you can access it regularly to remind yourself of your purpose in life.

CASE SCENARIOS

1. In Jennifer's literature class, she is reading Tim O'Brien's novel *The Things They Carried*. Although she understands that the novel is about the Vietnam War, she doesn't know why she has to read a book that contains so much profanity and graphic images of death. Jennifer has made an appointment to speak to her professor about the assignment, because she wants to get out of reading a book that is so depressing and discomforting. She is prepared to suggest that she read and write a paper on a Shakespearean play instead—a paper that she did in high school and got an A on.

    Use the following scale to rate the decision that has been made (1 = Poor Decision, 5 = Excellent Decision). Be prepared to explain your answer.

    Poor Decision ← 1 —— 2 —— 3 —— 4 —— 5 → Excellent Decision

2. Jai-Ling is taking a biology class. One of her assignments is to create a group presentation on an assigned topic. Her group's topic is the theory of evolution, a theory that Jai-Ling finds fascinating, even though all she knows about it is what little she learned in high school. When Jai-Ling meets with her group to begin work on the presentation, two group members express deep concern about being asked to study something that they don't believe in. They refuse to help with the project, even though they know their lack of participation will lower the whole group's grade. Jai-Ling tells these group members that they are being immature and ridiculous, because one of the purposes of being in college is to be challenged in one's thinking. She goes straight to the professor to complain and to ask to be assigned to a new group.

    Use the following scale to rate the decision that has been made (1 = Poor Decision, 5 = Excellent Decision). Be prepared to explain your answer.

    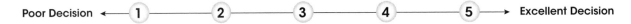

    Poor Decision ← 1 —— 2 —— 3 —— 4 —— 5 → Excellent Decision

3. Paul has just started college and is surprised by some of his professors' expectations. One professor told the class that she didn't care if they attended or not; she would post all the lectures, notes, answers to homework, and study guides online. Another class has 300 students, and Paul feels lost in the sea of fellow classmates. Only his first-year orientation class is small, and that professor demands that he attend regularly. A couple of Paul's classmates have approached him about taking turns attending classes and sharing notes. He will attend one week, and the two classmates will attend the following two weeks. Paul won't have to attend some of his classes for two weeks, which will allow him more time to do other things, like work and get involved in student activities. Because two of Paul's professors don't take attendance and won't know if he attends class, he decides to agree to the arrangement.

    Use the following scale to rate the decision that has been made (1 = Poor Decision, 5 = Excellent Decision). Be prepared to explain your answer.

    Poor Decision ← 1 —— 2 —— 3 —— 4 —— 5 → Excellent Decision

Take It with You

Action Item	Deadline	First Step
Review and update your Five "Whys?" for being in college (Activity 1) every term.		
Review and update your Who's in Your Circle? diagram (Activity 2) twice a year.		
Review and update your Three S.M.A.R.T Goals for the Semester (Activity 3) every term.		
Write your Personal Mission Statement (Activity 4).		

REFERENCE

Barro, R. J., & Lee, J. (2010). *A new data set of educational attainment in the world, 1950–2010.* Retrieved from http://www.nber.org/papers/w15902.pdf

2 Time Management

Pouring her fourth cup of coffee at 11:00 P.M., Laura searched for the history paper assignment that her professor had handed out a month ago. It was due at 9:00 A.M. tomorrow, and she was just getting started.

Laura sank into her chair at the kitchen table to go through her backpack one more time and debated whether to call a classmate for help. Was it too late to call? She sent a text to Michael, a classmate who always seemed to be organized, and waited for his response.

Laura didn't normally procrastinate about her schoolwork, but her youngest child had been sick for two days and she had been at home caring for him. She also wasn't sure what topic to write about in her paper. When Michael had sent a message three days ago that he'd completed the paper, she hadn't worried too much about her ability to get it done.

After three hours of intense work, Laura finished the paper. It wasn't perfect, but it was the required "at least eight pages in length" and on topic. Her eyes were too tired to proofread the paper after finishing it, but she decided to print it out before going to bed.

"I hope Professor Mallick doesn't read these papers very carefully," Laura said to herself as she began printing out the paper. Then the loud screech of the printer got her attention! She knew the screech meant that she wouldn't be able to print out and review her paper at home. She'd have to go to campus early and try to find a working printer before her class. Right now, she just wanted to get a couple hours of sleep.

As you read Laura's story, you probably picked up on the key idea that a lot of the stress she's facing about her assignment is due to her own procrastination and lack of planning. As you step into college, you may face similar challenges.

To help you become a better time manager, this chapter will help you learn how to do the following:

- Develop an effective time-management strategy.
- Prioritize your activities.
- Make the best use of various time-management tools.
- Avoid common time-management pitfalls.

LEARNING OUTCOME

Create an academic time-management plan.

MyStudentSuccessLab (www.mystudentsuccesslab.com) is an online solution designed to help you 'Start strong, Finish stronger' by building skills for ongoing personal and professional development.

NOW IS THE TIME TO DEVELOP AN EFFECTIVE TIME-MANAGEMENT STRATEGY

The number-one issue that college students say is their biggest challenge is time management. Why?

- **The college experience adds new and different responsibilities to an already busy life.** Even before you stepped onto campus, you probably felt like your life was busy. Now, you are going to college full time on top of having a full-time life.

- **The college experience brings high expectations.** As a highly motivated, success-oriented person, you have already placed high expectations on yourself. Now, in addition to your own expectations, your professors, advisors, parents, and other people who care about you will have expectations for you to succeed.

- **The college experience includes a wide variety of responsibilities.** As a full-time student, you're taking three to five different classes—each with its own requirements and schedule. You may also be involved in clubs or other student organizations and working and juggling family and social responsibilities, as well.

- **The college experience puts you in charge.** You have far more autonomy to make decisions about how you spend your time in college than you did previously in high school or at work. Having this freedom can be exciting, but it also brings a new level of responsibility for managing your time without direct supervision from your parents, teachers, or employer.

To face the time-management challenge, you need to develop an effective time-management strategy. An effective strategy will help you be productive (get a lot done), effective (do it well), and satisfied (feel good about it) in your personal and academic lives.

One of the main reasons having an effective time-management strategy helps you feel satisfied is that it helps you feel in control. As explained by Nelson and Low (2010, pp. 100–101) in their book about emotional intelligence, "An important by-product of good time management is a feeling of self-control—we are managing our responsibilities, not being managed by them." You will certainly feel more in control of your time after you complete this chapter!

Your time-management strategy is your plan for using your most valuable resource—your time—to fulfill your personal mission statement and to achieve your goals (SMART goals, of course!). How you use your time and organize your activities will depend on your goals (such as completing your degree, securing a job, and building relationships) and your personal mission statement (which defines your values and purpose in life). For example, if your personal mission statement places a high level of importance on helping others and giving back to society, then your allocation of time to activities that reflect those values should be consistent.

Throughout this chapter, be sure to keep your goals and mission statement in sight, as they should serve as the compass that guides your time-management decisions.

KNOW YOUR PRIORITIES

You may already have some kind of system for keeping track of all the various tasks you have to complete, activities you need to attend, and people you need to contact. Items like these typically end up on your to-do list or a scattered selection of sticky notes posted around your dorm room or car interior.

Meeting EXPECTATIONS

The college will expect that I ...	To meet that expectation, I will ...
Example: . . . turn in assignments on time.	Example: . . . post assignments on my calendar system as soon as I get them and schedule blocks of time on my calendar well before assignment due dates to start working on them.

You also know from experience that not every responsibility or activity on your list is of equal importance. To be successful in school and in life, you need to focus on the most important (and not necessarily the most urgent) responsibilities and activities.

Some responsibilities and activities might be urgent but not important, while others may be important but not urgent. An urgent responsibility or activity tries to demand your time and energy right now. For instance, suppose that your friends are texting you to make plans for the evening, and they want you to reply right away. But at the moment, you're devoting your attention to developing long-term goals and writing a personal mission statement. What should you do: reply to the text message or keep working?

Making this decision requires distinguishing between the urgent and the important—something you do hundreds of times every day. The more you keep your focus on achieving what's important and keeping what's urgent within manageable limits, the more success you will experience.

Distinguishing between the urgent and the important will help you engage in an important activity: prioritizing. A *priority* is something that is important and urgent at the moment. *Prioritizing* is the act of ranking or sorting responsibilities and activities from most important to least important to help you decide what to do, at what time, and what to work on first.

As you step into the college experience, the number of activities and responsibilities competing for your time and attention will quickly multiply. Your ability to prioritize will be critically important to your success. You will need to continually review the list of activities and responsibilities in your life and keep them ranked according to their importance.

Here's an example of a prioritization strategy you may want to try. Look at the syllabus from one of the classes you're taking this semester, and find the "Grading" section. Professors typically provide information about how

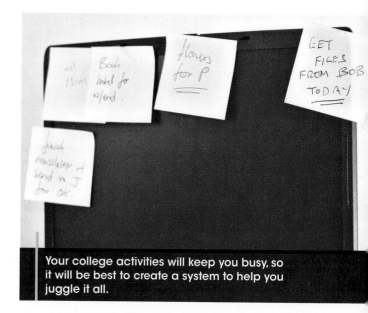

Your college activities will keep you busy, so it will be best to create a system to help you juggle it all.

It's in the SYLLABUS

Look at the syllabus for each course you're taking to help determine your priorities and tasks for each week of the semester. Record the due dates for all of your assignments in all of your classes in a single calendar system. Chances are, deadlines will overlap some weeks, and you'll find yourself needing to take an exam and finish a project in the same week. By planning ahead, you can work on some of these assignments ahead of time, thereby avoiding having to complete several important projects at once. Also think about these questions:

- How much time do you anticipate spending on each course?
- What days or weeks will be particularly busy for you?
- What additional obligations will you have during those busy times?
- How will you manage your priorities and time?

they will determine grades in their classes, including percentages or point values of individual assignments, quizzes, exams, and projects that make up a student's total grade. For instance, the final exam in your calculus course might account for 25% of your grade, whereas one of the quizzes might be worth 3%. Which of these two is most important? Clearly, because the final exam contributes far more to your grade than an individual quiz, the exam is more important (assuming that you're looking at the issue primarily in terms of your grade). Comparing individual assignments, projects, and exams on the basis of their value or contribution to your total grade is one useful technique that can help you prioritize your work.

Deadlines, of course, are another important consideration in prioritizing. In general, an assignment or responsibility that has an immediate deadline should be a higher priority than one that's due later. But also be sure to differentiate between the urgent and the important. If you focus only on those responsibilities that have near-term deadlines, then you won't have much time to work on activities that are more important, such as setting long-term goals and conducting research to help you plan your career. One approach to meeting this challenge is to give yourself a fixed amount of time each day to tackle the urgent issues in your life, while also scheduling time for important but not urgent activities.

USING TOOLS CAN HELP YOU MANAGE TIME

As you implement your time-management strategy, you can draw on a wide variety of tools to help you achieve your goals.

Calendars, Lists, and Workspaces

If you prefer to use a paper calendar, you have several different types to choose from: daily, weekly, and monthly. Once you determine the type that works best for you, make a habit of writing down the tasks you need to do, no matter how big or small. Here's an example of a typical list of a day's activities for a student like Laura:

Thursday
- Make appointment to have oil changed.
- Pick up medicine for Mom.
- Turn in housing deposit for next semester.
- Study for history quiz on Friday.
- Write essay for English composition.
- Turn in student club membership application.

A typical monthly calendar allows you to see several weeks at once, so that you can be aware of upcoming events. Often, however, there is little space on a monthly calendar to write down detailed information, such as Laura's activity list.

A weekly calendar allows you to glance at one week at a time. The key benefit of a weekly calendar is that it gives you room to write out the details of specific activities. However, a key drawback of a weekly calendar is that you won't be able to look ahead at what you have to do in the next week or two.

A daily calendar usually provides the most space to write day-to-day tasks and appointments. This kind of calendar may be the most difficult to work with, though, if you need to plan ahead. Since you can't see the rest of the week or month, you may overlook important events or be surprised by them. Use a daily calendar if you are extremely organized and can plan ahead effectively, or use it in addition to a monthly calendar.

If you have reliable Internet access in your home, apartment, or dorm, and access to a computer while on campus, consider using a web-based electronic calendar system and priority list. Also consider using your phone's calendar to help you stay on track. In many cases, your phone calendar can be synced to your computer calendar, which will allow you to stay updated no matter what device or devices you use. An electronic calendar allows you to set up events to automatically repeat themselves (for example, "Calculus quiz every Thursday"; "Dad's birthday on March 18"), to revise priority lists without having to rewrite them, to set up reminders and alerts that prompt you about upcoming deadlines and events, and to share your calendar with others so you can coordinate team projects and family responsibilities. The added benefit of a web-based system is that you can access it anytime and anywhere you have Internet access.

Once you've chosen the calendar system that works best for you, find your university's academic calendar on the campus website or in the catalog, and add the following important dates to your schedule:

Checklist of Important Dates
_____ Deadlines for registering and filing financial aid forms
_____ Date for the beginning of classes (or instruction)
_____ Drop/add dates for changing class schedule
_____ Due dates for paying tuition and fees
_____ Withdrawal dates for leaving college before semester is over
_____ Registration dates for next semester
_____ Holidays or breaks within the semester and between semesters

Deciding on the ideal calendar and creating a priority list are the first steps to managing your time well, but there is more you can do. Creating a quiet, clutter-free space where you can study and complete assignments will also help you manage your time effectively and efficiently. If you don't have a place in your house or apartment that you can call your own, try to set up a comfortable chair at the kitchen table. Make sure your workspace is comfortable and quiet and has adequate space for books, notebooks, and other supplies. It has to be a place that you want to be, or you will find it difficult to go there and stay on task.

Routines Are Time-Management Tools

Once you've set up an effective calendar and priority list, you can start to establish a time-management routine that helps you stay on track and maintain control over your life. For your calendar and task list to be effective, you need to establish the daily routine of reviewing and updating this information. Take a few minutes every evening to review what you've accomplished and to check off those items from your priority list (this will be a very satisfying experience!), to add new tasks that come up during the day, and to review tomorrow's calendar and priority list so you can anticipate tomorrow's goals.

Knowing what to expect during the day will make surprises less likely. Also, if you know that you have an early start tomorrow, you can make special preparations the night

THE UNWRITTEN RULES
Of Time Management

- **Projects, papers, and exams all tend to collide at the same time each term.** The best way not only to survive but also to succeed each term is to start early on your projects and assignments. Also be sure to review your notes and class materials each week so that studying for midterms and finals won't require as much time or effort.

- **The best times to accomplish important items on your priority list may come between terms.** Look for opportunities during spring break, holiday breaks, summer, and even three-day weekends to enjoy some peace and quiet and to revisit the important-but-not-urgent items on your list (for example, your personal mission statement, SMART goals, and career plan).

- **No matter how well you think you can work under pressure, your professors will detect procrastination.** As soon as a professor sees evidence of your procrastination, you'll be at a disadvantage. Most important, if you wait too long to start or complete an assignment, you'll forego the biggest advantage of getting an early start: the opportunity to get helpful feedback from your professor on preliminary drafts of your work. According to Beck (2012), "Too much stress, fatigue, and time pressure can kill creativity: A little bit of stress might help to get you motivated, but too much of it will typically cause you to shut down."

- **Even with today's technology, it takes time to learn.** In a comprehensive study of student success, chronicled in the book *What Matters in College*, Astin (1997) notes that the amount of time students spend practicing what they are trying to learn (or "time on task") is *the* single greatest predictor of academic success. Sorry, no shortcuts here!

before, such as packing your lunch, organizing your backpack, looking at a map to make sure you know where you have to go, and setting your alarm (and a back-up, if you tend to hit the snooze button a lot!). Having a stressful morning tends to start you on the wrong track for the day. Try to avoid the stress with some thoughtful planning the night before.

The second element of your time-management routine that can help you reduce your stress and put you in control of your schedule is a strategy called *back planning*. The basic idea of back planning is to look ahead to the deadline for a task, estimate the amount of time it will take to complete the task, and then establish a starting point for the task. For example, if you know that you need to write a 20-page paper for English composition and you expect that all of the research, writing, editing, formatting, and printing will take two weeks, then you can schedule time to start the project at least two weeks before its deadline.

Back planning works for short-term planning, too. If you know that your morning class starts at 8:30 A.M. and it typically takes 45 minutes for you to complete your entire morning routine and find parking, then you know that you need to walk out the door of your dorm or apartment no later than 7:45 A.M. to be on time. Establishing these short-term and long-term milestones will help you stay on track to meet deadlines and reduce the stress that's often associated with running behind.

LOOKING OUT FOR TIME-MANAGEMENT PITFALLS

Avoid the "Black Holes" of Technology and Procrastination

Often portrayed in science fiction movies or scientific documentaries, black holes in space absorb everything around them, including light. From the perspective of managing your time and energy, television, video games, and social media (such as Facebook and Twitter) have the potential to be virtual black holes in your life. You may plan on watching television for only 10 minutes, but chances are good that you'll still be sitting in front of the screen two hours later—and that you'll have accomplished nothing during that time. Playing video games has the capacity to be even more time consuming because of the interactive nature of today's games. Social media have emerged as yet another potential black hole, consuming both your time and attention by feeding continual distractions to you throughout the day.

As you establish strategies for managing your time and energy during your college experience, we urge extreme caution in your use of any of these items. All three are popular among college students, certainly, but if you don't use them in moderation, they will absorb your time and energy and leave little left over for your academic pursuits.

Indulging in media and technology are not the only ways to avoid doing your work in college. In fact, you'll most likely find a variety of ways to procrastinate. Cramming for quizzes and exams, pulling all-nighters to finish papers and projects, and missing work or skipping classes to finish assignments on time are all examples of procrastination. Any type of last-minute, hurried effort to meet a deadline tends to produce relatively poor academic performance and to cause a tremendous amount of emotional, physical, and social stress. However, using these desperate strategies is avoidable! With effective back planning, you can eliminate the need to stay up all night before an exam or to miss other classes to finish an assignment.

While it may seem like you can multitask and stay on track with your college work, you may find it more difficult to stay focused and complete tasks with so many distractions.

To avoid procrastination, the single biggest obstacle you need to overcome is putting off starting the project. Procrastination typically occurs when we (yes, professors sometimes procrastinate, too) are confused, intimidated, or overwhelmed by an assignment or task. Our fear gets the best of us, and we choose to forget about the assignment for a while, instead of trying to get started on it. Once we do get started, our fear tends to go away, and we discover that we're making more progress than we had expected.

In addition to risking running short of time, procrastinators face another problem: When the fear of missing the deadline and being late begins to creep in, they lose their ability to be clear thinkers and creative problem solvers. If you've ever been pressed to remember a phone number, locker combination, or other mental detail, you've probably discovered that it's more difficult to think clearly and solve problems when you're in a hurry. In the same way, it's difficult to be thoughtful and creative when you're trying to study for an exam or write a paper under time pressure.

We've spent a lot of time on procrastination, because it's such a common phenomenon in college and we see our students suffering unnecessary consequences from it. When you are assigned homework, projects, or papers, use back planning to clearly establish your start date for the project, as well as important milestones along the way (for example, "Read first two chapters by September 15"). Build those milestones into your calendar system, set time aside to do the work, and get started. If you establish the routine of regularly reviewing your calendar and to-do list and using back planning, you'll take control of your time and develop skills that will serve you well in college and throughout your life.

Multitask in Moderation

The ability to *multitask*—that is, to manage several activities or to pay attention to more than one task at a time—is often praised as an admirable and even necessary skill. In fact, many people believe that you can get more done and be more productive by multitasking than by doing one thing at a time. However, the scientific evidence doesn't support this common belief. In the article "Manage Your Energy, Not Your Time," Schwartz (2007, p. 67) explains:

> Many executives view multitasking as a necessity in the face of all the demands they juggle, but it actually undermines productivity. Distractions are costly: A temporary shift in attention from one task to another—stopping to answer an e-mail or take a phone call, for instance—increases the amount of time necessary to finish the primary task by as much as 25%, a phenomenon known as "switching time." It's far more efficient to fully focus for 90 to 120 minutes, take a true break, and then fully focus on the next activity.

If you tend to check your email, respond to text messages, monitor your Facebook status, and listen to your iPod while attempting to write a paper, study for an exam, or organize your calendar, you are undermining your ability to perform well, because performing these simultaneous tasks saps both your time and energy. Shut down the peripheral activities and stimuli and focus on the primary task at hand, and you'll find yourself accomplishing far more than you expected.

Manage Your Energy

Just as important as managing your time is managing your energy. Think about this scenario: You have the entire weekend off from work, and your spouse has taken the kids to visit their grandparents. That means you have 48 hours of complete solitude to write a research paper that's due on Monday. Sounds ideal, doesn't it? But what if you have the flu for those two days? And does having the time mean anything when you don't have the energy to do the work? What if you've just pulled two double shifts and haven't slept more than five hours in the past two days? Will you be able to use your free 48 hours productively, or will you need to take care of yourself?

INTEGRITY *Matters*

Do you tend to use your smartphone or another electronic device at the same time you're talking to someone in person? If so, you should know that this type of behavior may be considered rude and disrespectful by professors and college staff and is even an issue of personal integrity. Why? You're signaling to that person that he or she isn't important enough to warrant your full attention. One way to maintain integrity—and demonstrate respect—is to turn off your cell phone and put it in your backpack when you visit with a professor during office hours and when you attend class.

YOUR TURN

In approximately 250 words, describe how you feel when others haven't given you their undivided attention when you've wanted it.

Time is only valuable if you have the energy to use it well. Energy includes both physical and mental sharpness. We all experience variations in how sharp we feel throughout the day. Researchers sometimes refer to this as our *circadian rhythm*. The key is to understand yourself well enough to know when you are at the peak of your mental and physical alertness and when you are not.

In addition to falling and rising throughout the day, your energy level falls and rises throughout the week. Do you find yourself tired on Monday mornings but full of energy on Fridays? Or do you feel worn out by Thursday evenings but rejuvenated on Sundays? Depending on your work, school, and personal schedules, you'll find that you have regular bursts of energy at certain times of the week.

Once you've identified the hours in the day and the days in the week when you tend to be at your best, you can build your schedule to maximize your productivity during those times. You can also schedule activities that don't require as much effort or concentration during times when you aren't at your peak performance. Schedule activities such as writing papers, solving complex math problems, and reading assigned articles and books for peak times. It's also during these times that you'll most need your quiet, uncluttered workspace. Arranging your schedule and workspace will require some discipline and advanced planning, because you'll be tempted by other tasks and distractions. Most students are at or near the peak of their mental alertness shortly after waking up in the morning.

Getting and staying organized will help you manage your time well.

What should you do during those times when you aren't at your peak? First of all, recognize that it's OK to take breaks from working hard. In fact, it's actually more productive to take breaks than to try to work hard all day. The good news is that even when you don't feel mentally or physically sharp, you can still accomplish a lot. During those times, perform the common "time zappers" that can rob college students of their time: reviewing and sending emails, making phone calls, running errands, preparing meals, talking with roommates, taking a walk or swimming laps, or doing a form of meditative exercise.

Another way to help manage your energy is to become aware of what activities help you relax when you are stressed and what activities allow you to refill your energy reserves when you are dragging. If an activity rejuvenates you and helps you recharge, you may want to schedule it for times when you need to build up energy. If an activity helps you wind down, you may want to schedule it for after you have completed a major task.

CASE SCENARIOS

1. Janice has been doing very well in her classes. She has been able to manage her time wisely and adjust her schedule whenever something unexpected has come up. But this week promises to be hectic! Janet's boss expects her to stay late every day to finish a special project; she has an important exam on Thursday evening; her daughter has just come down with a stomach virus; and her husband will be out of town until late Friday. Janice's goal is to take care of each task without jeopardizing her job, her grade, or her daughter's welfare, but she knows that she can't realistically handle all these things. She decides to ask her professor if she can take the exam the following week, after finishing her boss's special project, and she asks a good friend to take care of her daughter so that she can work late every day until she finishes the project. At this point, Janice's top priority is her job.

   Use the following scale to rate the decision that has been made (1 = Poor Decision, 5 = Excellent Decision). Be prepared to explain your answer.

   Poor Decision ← ①——②——③——④——⑤ → Excellent Decision

2. Glenn is a constant procrastinator. He feeds on the adrenaline that rushes through his body when he waits until the last minute to complete an assignment. However, the last time he did this, which was for his computer programming class, he ended up failing the assignment because he ran out of time. Then, he was exhausted for three days because he had stayed up for 36 hours straight. Glenn really wants to break his procrastination habit, so he's created a study group, in which he works together with classmates on assignments. For example, in his accounting class, each group member completes one of the homework questions, and then group members compile the answers to turn them in individually. Glenn has also decided to borrow a friend's paper from a history class to use as the foundation for his own paper, so that he doesn't have to spend so much time starting from scratch.

   Use the following scale to rate the decision that has been made (1 = Poor Decision, 5 = Excellent Decision). Be prepared to explain your answer.

   Poor Decision ← ①——②——③——④——⑤ → Excellent Decision

3. Wanda was a good student in high school, taking Advanced Placement (AP) classes, making the honor roll, and being admitted to the National Honor Society. During her first four weeks of college, her classes have been easy, because they have covered material that she learned in her AP classes in high school. Looking ahead to next week, Wanda isn't worried that she has two tests and a paper due. The tests are in subjects she's familiar with, so she's planning to go over her lecture notes (she doesn't have many) the day before each test. The paper is due on Friday, so she's blocked off all of Thursday (after taking her second test) to complete it. Although she'll need to do research for the paper, she's confident that she can find what she needs searching the Internet on her laptop in her room.

   Use the following scale to rate the decision that has been made (1 = Poor Decision, 5 = Excellent Decision). Be prepared to explain your answer.

   Poor Decision ← ①——②——③——④——⑤ → Excellent Decision

Take It with You

Action Item	Deadline	First Step
Create your priority list for this week.		
Commit to a time each day to review and update your priority list and calendar.		
Reduce the "black holes" in your schedule.		
Identify and participate in activities that give you energy.		

REFERENCES

Astin, A. (1997). *What matters in college.* San Francisco: Jossey-Bass.

Beck, M. (2012, June 19). Anxiety can bring out the best. *Wall Street Journal,* pp. D1–D2.

Nelson, D., & Low, G. (2010). *Emotional intelligence: Achieving academic and career excellence.* Boston: Prentice Hall.

3 Money Management

Evan was on top of the world! At 20 years old, he had started college after working two years after high school. He had both real-life experience and a promising future, and he expected that going to college would be easier than working.

Evan had missed out on scholarships because he didn't enroll in college immediately after graduating from high school, but he had saved enough money to pay for the first two semesters and had received a grant that was based on his making good grades. He had also quit his full-time job so that he could concentrate on keeping his grades up.

What Evan didn't expect, however, were the extra costs of college: books, computers, and extra course materials.

"Have you ever worked for a moving company on the weekends?" he asked a classmate named Juanita, who seemed to be in the same position he was—looking for ways to make money.

"No," she said, "but I signed up to be a subject in a research study with the psychology department. I made $50."

"That would pay for that extra book that we have to buy in sociology," Evan noted. "I didn't think we really had to have it, but I guess I was wrong."

"I get everything on the syllabus—whether the professor mentions it the first day of class or not," said Juanita.

Evan had been trying to get by without buying everything his professors had listed as required for the course. He had planned either to borrow extra books or to try to find them in the library. But he had already missed some important assignments because he didn't have what he needed to do them.

"The psych department has another study coming up," Juanita added. "It's a sleep deprivation study, and each participant will get paid $120."

Evan asked Juanita where he could find out more information. He would definitely sign up for this study!

Like Evan and Juanita, you may face financial responsibilities and challenges that you didn't anticipate when you were first accepted into college. To help you prepare for those responsibilities and challenges, this chapter will help you do the following:

- Develop financial literacy.
- Set financial goals.
- Develop strategies for managing your finances.
- Evaluate the advantages and disadvantages of using credit.

LEARNING OUTCOME

Create long-term and short-term financial goals.

FINANCIAL LITERACY IS A LIFELONG LESSON

Budgeting your money for college expenses will be crucial to your staying in college and being less stressed.

For many college students, meeting the academic expectations of higher education isn't their greatest challenge. Rather, they struggle with handling the financial issues that go along with the college experience. Some students choose to go to school full time and do not work, while others juggle a job—either part time or full time—while going to school. No matter what their financial situation, many students add the expense of going to college to their other obligations, or they use grants, loans, or scholarships to cover costs.

You have successfully enrolled in college, so you already know that investing in your future takes more than courage. It also takes cash—or at least access to funds to cover the costs. Unfortunately, the costs of college continue to rise and will likely continue rising with each passing year.

So, what can you do? The first step is to develop *financial literacy*. That means that you have the knowledge about finances you need to make important decisions, and that you have skills to manage your financial resources effectively. It's not enough to know a lot about money. You also need to apply that knowledge to your daily habits and decision making. To get started, it's important to identify all of the various costs that are associated with college and to build a budget for managing your finances during your college years.

Estimate Your College Costs

Estimating what you're going to spend for your college education is a great first step toward becoming financially literate. Estimating will also help you with budgeting.

Since this is your first time in college, it will be helpful to see what you can expect to spend as you work on and complete your degree. The following list points out typical college expenses:

- **Fees and tuition:** These expenses are what you pay for the classes you take. The amount you pay may vary based on the number of units or hours you're taking, whether you are an in-state or out-of-state student, whether you're an undergraduate or graduate student, and perhaps even based on your program or major.

- **Books and supplies:** For most of the courses you'll take in college, you'll be required to purchase a textbook, a workbook, and perhaps other supplies. In college, you'll be responsible for buying these items and bringing them to class. In addition to textbooks, you may also need to purchase notebooks or binders, a laptop or desktop computer, a backpack, paper (for notes and for printing), pens and pencils, a calculator, computer software, a jump drive or flash drive (for storing and transferring electronic files), a stapler, a hole punch, and a ruler. In addition, you may need to buy specialized supplies for labs or classes such as photography and drawing.

- **Room and board:** *Room* is the cost of your housing, such as on-campus housing in a dorm or off-campus housing in an apartment. *Board* is the cost of your meals. If you choose to live in a dorm, you may have the option to purchase a meal plan, which gives you a fixed amount of food each day at various cafeterias across campus. If you live off campus, board will be the cost of buying groceries and eating out.

- **Transportation:** Depending on your circumstances, you'll have expenses associated with getting yourself from where you live to campus, whether by car, motorcycle, bicycle, or public transportation. You may also have to pay fees for parking on campus.

- **Personal and miscellaneous:** This is a broad category of costs that includes movies and entertainment, clothing, cell phone service, magazine subscriptions, and other daily expenses. Many of these expenses are easy to overlook unless you track them carefully.

You may also find other costs associated with going to college that aren't mentioned on your university's "Cost of Attendance" Web page or during new student orientation. Here are some examples:

- **Insurance:** Unless you're covered by your parents' medical insurance, you may need to pay for your own medical insurance or cover the costs of prescriptions and other medical expenses not covered by insurance.

- **Internet:** Having regular and reliable Internet access will create an additional monthly cost.

- **Child care:** If you are raising a child while going to college, you may need to pay for daycare or babysitting services.

Complete the Meeting Expectations exercise to begin thinking about what you can do to become financially literate.

It's in the SYLLABUS

Look at the syllabus for each course you're taking to determine what additional costs it might involve. Be sure to consider possible unstated or hidden costs, such as those involved in using a computer (printer supplies, Internet access, and so on). Also consider these questions:

- What will your textbooks and course materials cost?

- What will you have to pay for the use of technology?

- What unstated or hidden costs do you anticipate?

- How will you budget and pay for these costs?

Create a Budget

Once you've estimated all of the costs associated with going to college, you can create a monthly budget. A *budget* is a plan for matching how much money is needed to cover all costs with how much money is available. For this purpose, a budget has two main

Meeting EXPECTATIONS

The college will expect that I ...	To meet that expectation, I will ...
Example: . . . *pay for all the costs of college as they come due.*	Example: . . . *do research to learn about college cost estimates, talk to others in college to find out about hidden costs, and create a plan for having the money available when these costs are due.*

sections: income and expenses. The *income* section shows how much money you have available, whether from a job, savings, student loans, or other sources. The *expense* section shows your costs.

Although it may seem obvious, the fundamental rule of budgeting is that you can't spend more money than you have. And because certain expenses, such as tuition and car insurance, are paid only a few times a year, you need to have a method for putting money aside so the funds are available later to pay these relatively large bills.

Once you have estimated all your anticipated costs, creating a monthly budget can be relatively easy. The hard part is following it! First, you need to create a customized budget sheet. In the first column, estimate your income and expenses. Use the middle column to track your actual income and expenses each month. Record any differences in the final column by subtracting the actual amounts from the estimated amounts. For example, if you estimate that you earn $1,000 a month, but this month you earned $1,092, the difference is plus $92. If you earned $997, then the difference is minus $3. Comparing your budget to what actually happens each month will help you make adjustments and stay on track.

To figure out your monthly expenses and income, gather all your bills and pay-stubs. Organize them by category or type, and add up the numbers. It's a good idea to review at least three months' worth of bills to get an accurate picture of your expenses. If you have any bills that are paid less than once a month (say, every three months or six months), then you will need to convert them to monthly expenses. For example, if you pay $240 every six months for car insurance, then your monthly expense is $40 ($240 divided by six months).

One key to accurate budgeting is to be honest about your expenses. Write down everything you spend—even the money you spend on snacks and supplies. A good method for tracking your spending is to save every receipt from every purchase, organize them by category or type, and then total them each month. You may find that you spend $25 a week ($100 a month) on items that are unnecessary. The better you can track unnecessary items, the better you can control your spending.

Learn More about Your Finances

Developing financial literacy is a lifelong learning opportunity. You started learning some important lessons about money when you were very young, and now you have a chance to learn even more by navigating the costs of college. You can explore financial matters further by consulting the numerous resources that are available to you. Many local, state, and federal government programs provide free information and counseling for individuals who are interested in getting their finances on track. In addition, your local library and bookstore offer many good resources on money management and financial matters.

Set Financial Goals to Help Stay on Track

After you get an accurate picture of your income and expenses and have planned a monthly budget, you can start setting short-term and long-term financial goals. Setting goals can help you fulfill your personal mission statement, live according to your values, and achieve the success that defines your purpose. Financial goals are an important part of your personal mission, because they help you determine if you're reaching the milestones you know are necessary to achieve long-term success.

You should set both short-term and long-term financial goals. *Short-term goals* apply to the next 12 months of your life. For example, your first short-term goal might be tracking your monthly budget and consistently spending 5% less than you earn. Another short-term goal might be to put enough money in your savings account each month to

THE UNWRITTEN RULES
Of Money Management

- **The financial aid package the university offers you may include loans, but remember that loans must be paid back.** Sometimes, the financial aid package or offer makes it seem as though you have to pay very little out of pocket for college. Look carefully, however, to see what parts of the costs are being covered by loans, because that's the part you'll have to pay back—with interest.

- **When applying for part-time jobs, internships, and work study opportunities, be ahead of the game.** Talk to someone in the career advising center or stop by several local employers and ask when they typically see a large number of students putting their resumes together and applying for jobs. Plan on getting your applications in before that time.

- **Explore the range of academic options that are becoming available in higher education.** With your academic plan in hand and full knowledge of the courses you need to take to complete your degree, be a savvy student. Be aware of all your options for earning those credits. For example, if you're attending a four-year university, you may be able to take general education courses at a local community college online or over the summer. These courses are often accepted as substitutes by four-year universities.

- **Make every course count.** If your college budget is tight, you need to make sure that every course you take will apply toward your degree. Sometimes, students take an unnecessary class because they don't like the time or day when a class they need for their degree is offered.

- **Keep in mind that the best-paying college jobs are sometimes the least glamorous.** College students are often attracted to high-visibility jobs, like bartending in a popular club or merchandising in a trendy store. Don't pass up jobs that pay a lot more and offer better work experience but aren't perceived as popular or cool. Look for jobs at distribution centers, daycares, cleaning and maintenance services, local factories, and telephone-based customer service companies. These jobs may be advertised in "Help Wanted" or "Temporary Hire" listings online or through a "temp" employment agency in your area.

pay for your study-abroad experience next year. Because your budget is the product of both income and expenses, your short-term goals might apply to either. For example, if you want to save $1,000 by next summer to buy a new computer, you should set short-term goals for both earning extra income and reducing your expenses.

Long-term goals apply to the next two to five years and even beyond. Your long-term goals can be extensions of your short-term goals. For example, you may set a long-term goal to pay for college without having to take out student loans. Your long-term goal of avoiding student loans will be met only if you can meet your short-term goal of keeping your expenses below your income every month.

Financial goals are an important part of your personal mission statement. They can also serve as useful guides and powerful motivators to help you make the decisions, day after day and week after week, that are necessary to achieving your purpose in life.

Complete Activity 1, Setting SMART Financial Goals, to write out some of your financial goals.

There are many scholarships that go unclaimed each year. Look for ones that you qualify for and apply!

ACTIVITY 1   Setting SMART Financial Goals

Use the SMART approach you learned in Chapter 1 (specific, measurable, achievable, realistic, time specific) to write financial goals for your first term, your first year, and all four years of your college experience. Then identify someone you added to your Who's in Your Circle? chart (Activity 2 in Chapter 1) that you can share and discuss these goals with and that can help you stay on track to achieve them.

HAVING A GOOD STRATEGY CAN HELP YOU MANAGE YOUR FINANCES

A good financial plan is only useful if you stick to it. The following tips can help you increase your financial literacy "muscles," especially if you exercise them regularly:

- **Balance your checkbook and other accounts every month.** If you're comfortable managing your finances on a computer, you'll find it helpful to use software programs and online tools like Quicken and Mint.com. If you're just getting started, use a simple tool, such as an Excel spreadsheet or even a paper-and-pencil monthly budget-tracking form.
- **Compare your bank's financial statements with your own recording of expenses and income.** Doing this will help you catch any unauthorized charges on your account or bank fees that were posted inappropriately.
- **Separate your bills from other mail, and create a schedule for paying them.** Your paper-based or electronic calendar system is ideal for this scheduling purpose. Most bills are due on the same day each month, so you can set up recurring reminders to pay them.
- **Sign up to pay your bills online if it's possible and easier to pay them this way.** Be sure, however, that you have reliable Internet access, and use a consistent email address so you don't lose track of these transactions.
- **If you have a credit card, use it for emergencies only.** Resist the temptation to use your credit card for everyday expenses.
- **To prepare for unexpected expenses, save a small percentage of your monthly income in a separate account.** For example, for every $100 you earn, put $5 (5%) in an emergency savings account. Make it a goal to increase your savings percentage over time.
- **Check the university's website every semester for information about changes in tuition and fees.** Keep yourself informed about expected expenses from semester to semester.

Protect Yourself

Budgeting and creating a plan aren't quite enough to make sure that you're on a firm financial foundation. You also need to protect yourself from various financial scams, which can do more harm than just drain your bank account. If something sounds too good to be true or doesn't seem quite right, it's quite possibly a scam.

Another risk that you have to manage is identity theft. Keep your bank cards in a safe, secure place at all times, and never, ever write down your ATM personal identification number (PIN) on a piece of paper. Also, be very cautious any time someone asks for your Social Security number. Never provide it in an email, and make sure that any form requesting this number is from an official authority, such as your college's financial aid office or registrar.

Know the Advantages and Disadvantages of Using Credit Cards

Why do some college students use credit cards instead of cash or checks to purchase items? There are two main reasons: One is that college students can't afford to pay outright for many things but want to buy them anyway, and the other is that paying with a credit card is very convenient.

INTEGRITY *Matters*

At some point during your college career, you may be invited to participate in a fraudulent or deceptive activity to generate extra money. The thought of taking part in something like this may seem farfetched to you at the moment, but you may face tough financial times during your college career that will make such an activity seem justifiable. If you ever find yourself in a difficult financial situation, seek advice from a financial aid officer or counselor at your university. Ask him or her to help you identify options and develop a solution.

YOUR TURN

In approximately 250 words, describe what you would do if you were offered the chance to make additional money for college but were unsure about the ethical issues involved. How would you decide what to do?

Students who rely on credit cards to make up for a lack of available funds tend to find themselves in financial trouble quickly. Credit cards typically carry high interest rates, and earning enough income to pay off accumulating debt is tough for most students. If you spend $1,000 using a credit card that charges 17% interest, and you make payments of $100 each month, you will be building more in interest than you will be paying each month. And that's assuming that you don't charge anything else!

If you're attracted to using a credit card because of the convenience, check with your current bank about getting a debit card. A debit card offers the same convenience as a credit card, but the funds for each purchase are withdrawn from your checking account, rather than loaned to you. This distinctive feature of a debit card can help you avoid going into debt and paying high interest charges—problems that have devastated many students.

OPTIONS FOR PAYING FOR COLLEGE

When thinking about the issues that will affect your financial future, paying for college will likely be at the top of your list. Even if you have a solid plan for paying tuition, fees, and books, it's worth your time to investigate other methods, in case your current plan falls through.

Scholarships

Winning a scholarship is by far the most rewarding way to pay for college—financially and psychologically. A scholarship is literally free money. You don't have to pay it back. Thousands of scholarships are available for both financially needy and academically accomplished students, but hard work is often needed to find them. To find the scholarships that match your profile, get the word out to friends and family that you are looking.

Another way to get information about scholarships is to talk with the financial aid officers and counselors at your college. They have knowledge of and access to scholarships that fit their college's student profiles, such as single-parent and transfer

Being able finance your college degree will help you achieve your dreams.

scholarships, and that will pay tuition and fees at a four-year university. Other effective methods for finding scholarships are to investigate sources at your library and to search the Internet. Searching print and web-based databases will provide you with more than enough information, but you'll need to narrow your focus to locate the options that best fit your qualities and circumstances.

Whatever information you find about scholarships—whether from books, in a counselor's office, or on the Internet—don't pay for it. No reputable scholarship will require applicants to pay a fee, and very few scholarship services will ask for payment. There are legitimate scholarship-searching services out there, but be careful. The web-site FinAid! (www.finaid.org) provides information about different types of financial aid for college students, as well as tips for avoiding scholarship service scams.

Grants

By definition, a *grant* is a form of financial assistance that doesn't need to be paid back. A common federal grant is the Pell Grant, which can be awarded for full-time or part-time enrollment.

To determine your eligibility for a grant, talk with your financial aid counselor or visit any of the various government websites that provide information about financial aid. When you research Pell Grants, you'll find that there is a maximum award ($5,500 for 2012–2013). You'll also find that your college will receive the money and then turn it over it to you once classes start. Because of new federal requirements about grants and student loans, colleges may wait several weeks before paying students. Don't expect to receive your grant the first day or week of classes, and be sure to make alternative arrangements to pay bills (including your bookstore bill).

Another type of grant is the Federal Supplemental Educational Opportunity Grant (FSEOG), which is available to students who demonstrate exceptional financial need.

According to the U.S. Department of Education (2012a), the difference between a Pell Grant and an FSEOG is that "each participating school will receive enough money to pay the Federal Pell Grants of its eligible students. There's no guarantee every eligible student will be able to receive an FSEOG." The procedure for receiving an FSEOG is similar to that for receiving a Pell Grant: Your eligibility will determine the amount you receive, and your college will give the money to you after the semester begins.

To remain eligible for a grant, you'll need to maintain good academic standing at your college. Be sure to make note of the minimum grade point average (GPA) that you must maintain to receive future grant money. And here's one last tip for staying eligible to receive grant funding: Make sure that you adhere to the college's attendance policy. If you miss too many classes or drop a class, you may be penalized and lose your grant or have to pay it back.

Student Loans

If you aren't eligible for grants or they don't pay enough to cover all your costs, then you should investigate student loans. The idea of taking out loans to attend college makes many students shudder with fear, because they don't want the added pressure of having to pay back what they borrow. If you can avoid taking out student loans, then by all means, do so. However, receiving student loans sometimes makes financial sense in the long run, if the alternative is to forego attending college.

Federal student loans typically charge low interest and can be paid back over 10 years. For a family that would have to drain their savings or borrow against their retirement or mortgage to pay for college, a low-interest student loan is a good option. Most loan programs allow students to *defer* (which means "to delay") payment until after they graduate, or students can sometimes defer payment if they remain unemployed after graduating. However, these loans may accumulate interest during the deferral period. Be sure to know the specific terms of your loan before making a decision about deferral.

One type of loan is the Stafford Loan, which comes in subsidized and unsubsidized versions. A *subsidized* loan is one in which the government pays the interest for you while you're in college. Once you graduate and start making payments on your loan, you'll accrue interest, as well. The government doesn't make interest payments for an *unsubsidized* loan. With this type of loan, you would need to decide whether to pay the interest while in college (usually a small amount) or allow the interest to be added (or *capitalized*) to the overall loan amount and wait until after you graduate to make any payments. This is a classic "pay now or pay more later" type of decision, which you need to think about carefully.

A federal Perkins Loan is a loan between you and your college. A Perkins Loan currently allows you to borrow $5,500 per year and up to $27,500 for five years, and you don't have to start repaying it until nine months after you graduate or drop below at least part-time student status (U.S. Department of Education, 2012b). One benefit of a Perkins Loan is that you may be able to cancel up to 100% of the debt if you meet certain criteria—for example, if you choose to teach in a "teacher shortage" area or serve as a full-time nurse following graduation.

Another method for receiving money to help pay for college is a PLUS (Parent Loan for Undergraduate Students). If you are fortunate enough to have parents who are willing to take out a loan to help you pay for college, then a PLUS is an option. For your parents to qualify, you must be a dependent student, which means your parents support you financially. Parents who take out a PLUS are usually trying to make up the difference between the cost of tuition and the financial aid package their child receives. Nonetheless, it's the parents who are ultimately responsible for repaying the loan, and repayment can begin as early as 60 days after receiving the loan.

CASE SCENARIOS

1. In addition to starting her second year of college, Korto is starting a new job. She needs money to pay for minor living expenses now that she has moved into an apartment by herself. Because Korto's financial aid has been delayed, she can't pay for both her apartment and her tuition and books at the beginning of the semester. Her college has offered to provide a monthly payment plan, but she has to complete her payments in three months. Korto isn't sure that's enough time, depending on whether her financial aid arrives by then. So she's decided to use a credit card to pay for her college expenses, because she knows she can afford at least the monthly minimum until her financial aid comes in.

    Use the following scale to rate the decision that has been made (1 = Poor Decision, 5 = Excellent Decision). Be prepared to explain your answer.

2. Jason has received a grant and a loan to pay his tuition and fees. He's taking 15 credit hours and has to keep a 2.5 GPA to remain eligible for both forms of financial aid. Unfortunately, Jason is failing a class, and the last day to drop a course this semester is the same day as a test in that class. Even though he has A's and B's in his other classes, he decides to drop the class before the exam to avoid lowering his GPA and putting his financial aid in jeopardy.

    Use the following scale to rate the decision that has been made (1 = Poor Decision, 5 = Excellent Decision). Be prepared to explain your answer.

3. Pauline is planning to transfer into a specialized program at her college. The new program involves additional costs, however, which she didn't plan on when she applied for financial aid and budgeted for the upcoming semester. The program advisor advises against students' working full time because of the academic demands of the program. Pauline has contacted a fee-based service that helps students find additional money to attend college. A good friend of hers used the service to get a private loan to complete her education. The service has said they will find money for Pauline, as well, to cover these unexpected costs.

    Use the following scale to rate the decision that has been made (1 = Poor Decision, 5 = Excellent Decision). Be prepared to explain your answer.

Take It with You

Action Item	Deadline	First Step
Create a monthly budget.	_____	_____
Develop SMART financial goals for your first term, first year, and four years of college.	_____	_____
Research your options for getting and using a debit card versus a credit card.	_____	_____
Identify all of your possible sources of funds for college.	_____	_____
_____	_____	_____

REFERENCES

U.S. Department of Education. (2012a). Types of Federal Student Aid. Retrieved from http://studentaid.ed.gov/sites/default/files/2012-13-funding-your-education.pdf

U.S. Department of Education. (2012b). Perkins Loans. Retrieved from http://studentaid.ed.gov/types/loans/perkin

4 Critical and Creative Thinking

Michael could hike 12 miles on a hot day in a sandstorm with 30 pounds of equipment on h back. What he couldn't do, he thought, was understand algebra.

Inside the student center, Michael sat down and opened his math notebook. He said to himse "The order of operations is F-O-I-L: first, outer, inner, last. But after that, I don't know what to do.

He wished the professor would just slow down and allow students to "get it" before moving c to the next unit. He was sure he wouldn't feel so stressed if the professor went at a slower pace

Michael had spent four years in the military and learned how to do all kinds of complicated task Algebra couldn't be as hard as most of what he'd learned.

"Maybe I'm not good at math and never will be," he thought. He had already failed a test, and eve though he wasn't doing all the homework, he felt he was doing enough to "get it."

Michael thought about what he could do to fix the problem: drop the class or study even more than the three hours a week h was already putting into the class? He decided to call his girlfriend, Lisa, to ask her opinion.

"Michael, do you remember when I struggled through biology?" she asked.

"Yeah, I do. I remember helping you study before you joined the study group," Michael told her.

"Well, don't forget that, first, I went to the tutoring center to get help with the class. One of the tutors helped me learn how to tak better notes and how to organize my studying time. Then you helped me practice before I felt confident enough to join a study group

"I know the tutoring center worked for you," Michael said, "but it's not my way of doing things. I can figure this out on my ow I hear they have some videos in the library that you can watch over and over until you get it. I'm heading there now. Bye. Michael turned off his phone and headed out of the student center and across campus to the library.

Like Michael, you will encounter situations in college that will challenge your ability to think critically and develop creative solutions. To prepare you for success in these situations, this chapter will help you do the following:

- Develop critical-thinking skills.
- Practice creative-thinking techniques.
- Appreciate the value of using critical-, analytical-, and creative-thinking skills to solve problems.

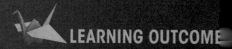

LEARNING OUTCOME

Solve a problem using critical and creative thinking.

MyStudentSuccessLab (www.mystudentsuccesslab.com) is an online solution designed to help you 'Start strong, Finish stronger' by building skills for ongoing personal and professional development.

CRITICAL-THINKING SKILLS WILL SERVE YOU WELL

Having strong critical-thinking skills will set you apart in both the classroom and the workplace: You'll be better informed, because you'll know how to find the information you need; you'll make better choices, because you'll understand your alternatives and their tradeoffs; and you'll continue to improve your decisions over time, because you'll learn from each new experience.

A *critical thinker* is "someone who uses specific criteria to evaluate reasoning and make decisions" (Diestler, 1998, p. 2). Someone who thinks critically doesn't take information at its face value. Instead, he or she carefully examines information for accuracy, authority, and logic before using it.

To illustrate the importance of using critical-thinking skills, consider this scenario:

> Michael receives an email message from his friend Juanita, who claims that she has unknowingly sent him a computer virus. Her email instructs him to search for the offending file and to delete it immediately. Unaware of any of the kinds of problems usually associated with viruses, Michael searches for the file and finds it—exactly where his friend said it would be on his computer. Juanita is a trustworthy person, and Michael values her advice, so he deletes the file. Then, the next day, he gets an email message from her that says she's sorry that the email she sent him was actually a hoax. That means Michael has deleted a perfectly normal file on his computer.

Now consider another scenario:

> Juanita sends Evan a link to a pop-up blocker, because she knows that he hates these annoying intrusions while surfing the Internet. Because Evan has been deceived by free software before, he decides to search several reputable sites that are devoted to reviewing new software. Evan finds that the pop-up blocker is a fraud. If he would've clicked on the link that Juanita sent him, his computer would have been overrun with pop-up advertisements of questionable origin.

In the first scenario, two people, at least, have been deceived by what appears to be legitimate and helpful information. Who doesn't want to rid his or her computer of a potentially dangerous virus? Unfortunately, Michael and his friend didn't question the information. In the second scenario, however, Evan checks out the information. He has encountered false claims before and knows that he must look into every piece of information that comes to him, regardless of whether it comes from a friendly source. Evan applied critical thinking to the

Finding and using resources on the Internet provides great opportunities for you to practice good critical-thinking skills.

It's in the SYLLABUS

As you review the detailed content of the syllabus from each class you're taking this semester, you'll find many places where critical-thinking skills will be important. Consider these questions:

- Will there be multiple-choice questions on quizzes and tests that challenge you to critically evaluate each answer option to select the "best" answer?
- Will you have to write term papers and reports that challenge you to find reliable sources of information to support your ideas?
- Find at least two other examples from your course syllabi that require critical thinking.

Meeting EXPECTATIONS

The college will expect that I ...	To meet that expectation, I will ...
Example: . . . *demonstrate critical–thinking skills in my classes and in every aspect of my college life.*	Example: . . . *gather and study information that will help me to evaluate my own beliefs and conclusions and the beliefs and conclusions of others.*
_____	_____
_____	_____
_____	_____
_____	_____

situation. Thinking critically allowed him to review the information he was sent and to search for authoritative sources that provided reliable information, so that he could make a decision about what action to take.

The two scenarios demonstrate the importance of critical thinking and how you can develop and practice critical-thinking skills for yourself. To think critically, you need to look for information that supports your own ideas and solutions and, with equal openness, look for information that supports ideas and solutions that are different from your own.

One of the best illustrations of applying critical thinking is reading a voter's guide. Use a search engine to locate your state's voter guide for an illustration of the format, which typically includes statements for and against the various propositions, and rebuttals to those statements. Voters who take the time to carefully review information on both sides of an argument are practicing critical thinking, because they are carefully evaluating both perspectives before making a final decision.

Critical-thinking skills, therefore, include the ability to identify your question or problem and to seek information from several sources and several points of view before making a decision or drawing a conclusion.

To practice critical-thinking skills and develop your ability to think critically, be on the lookout for situations in which knowing different perspectives or points of view might lead to new ideas or different conclusions. These situations might occur in class, in a club or Greek organizational activity, at work, with your roommates, or at home with your family. Also, practice your critical-thinking skills by doing Activity 1, Critical Thinking in Action.

ACTIVITY 1 Critical Thinking in Action

Write down three examples of situations that you can expect to encounter during your first term in college in which you can practice critical thinking. For example, will you study topics in some of your classes that might cause debate or disagreement between you and your professor or classmates? For each of the three examples, briefly describe how you can actively demonstrate critical thinking.

CREATIVE THINKING CAN HELP YOU DEVELOP NEW IDEAS

Creative thinking—or the act of creating ideas for solving problems—is an integral part of learning. Without creative thinking, there would be no inventions or new formulas, no breakthroughs in technology and science, no new art movements, no advances in design and architecture—the list is endless. Without creative thinking, there would be no electricity, no indoor plumbing, no automobiles, and no zippers. Just getting to your classes would be a totally different experience.

Creative thinking is a skill, a process, and an attitude (Harris, 2002, pp. 1–2). Put differently, creative thinkers aren't born with special powers of the imagination; rather, they use their imaginations more often than others. The good news is that you can learn to think creatively by following some of the basic guidelines shown in Exhibit 1, Questions to Generate Ideas.

Use the questions in Exhibit 1 to generate creative uses for the following objects:

Harris (2002, p. 5) states, "Creative thinking creates the ideas with which critical thinking works." To improve your creative abilities, ask the questions provided in Exhibit 1, maintain your curiosity about new ideas and perspectives, and spend time with people who have different backgrounds, experiences, and perspectives than your own.

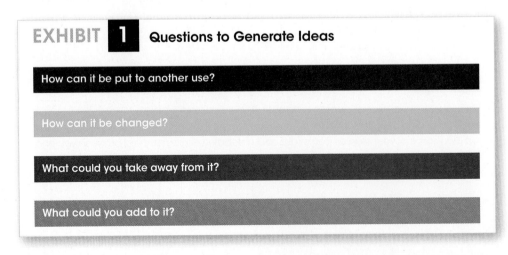

EXHIBIT 1 Questions to Generate Ideas

How can it be put to another use?

How can it be changed?

What could you take away from it?

What could you add to it?

CRITICAL AND CREATIVE THINKING CAN HELP YOU SOLVE PROBLEMS

Although not all critical thinking leads to problem solving, problem solving relies on critical thinking, as well as creative and analytical thinking. To think critically to solve a problem, you'll need to go through a process within a group or as an individual. Remember that the more minds that are working on a problem, the more likely that all sides of the problem will be addressed, which may make the solution that's reached better than if only one person works on the problem. You may not always have the opportunity to work in a group on a problem, but you may be able to ask others for their advice during the process.

Here are the basic steps of using critical thinking to solve a problem:

1. Identify the problem or goal.
2. Generate several possible solutions to the problem or goal.
3. Critically evaluate each possible solution.
4. Choose one solution and develop a plan for putting it in action.
5. Evaluate the solution after it's been in place for a while.

Exhibit 2, Creative-Thinking Strategies, Definitions, and Activities, provides more information about incorporating creative thinking into your everyday practice.

Creative and critical thinking are both important skills that will help you solve problems and create new solutions.

EXHIBIT 2 Creative-Thinking Strategies, Definitions, and Activities

Strategy	Definition	Activity
Try to improve your imagination each day.	Find ways to keep your mind sharp and your imagination flourishing. Turning off the TV and picking up a book is an easy way to stimulate your imagination. If you enjoy kinesthetic activities, create something to get your mind active.	Participate in one thinking or imaginative exercise each day, whether it's doing a crossword puzzle or Sudoku puzzle, constructing an object, or listing the plusses and minuses of the healthiness of what you ate for breakfast.
Consider what someone else would do.	Looking at a problem from a different perspective can provide you with more creative ideas.	Determine what topic or problem you want to generate more ideas for. Then choose two people—such as your mother and perhaps Oprah Winfrey or Walt Disney—and write down the different ways they would approach the issue.
Hold off on making judgments.	For creative thinking, evaluating or judging isn't necessary. Save it for critical thinking and problem solving.	Make a list of 50 ways to use a paper clip, and don't delete items or edit the list in any way. Share your list with others.

Step 1: Identify the Problem or Goal

Sometimes, the problem is obvious, and other times, we make incorrect assumptions about the real problem. Either way, it's important to take some time to clearly identify the problem before moving on to possible solutions.

For example, suppose you're constantly late for your first class every morning. You've might assumed it's because you're not getting up early enough. After examining the situation more closely, however, you discover that you're spending too much time trying to find a parking spot before class. The problem may actually be a transportation problem and not a problem with your sleeping habits.

Instead of trying to solve a problem, maybe you're trying to accomplish a particular goal. For example, maybe you want to set the goal to save an extra $200 over the next six months so you can buy an ebook reader.

Identifying the cause of a problem is the first logical step to take before you can begin to solve it. If you don't first identify the cause—or at least eliminate some of the possible causes—you won't solve the problem or you might create a whole new problem to solve.

Step 2: Generate Several Possible Solutions

This is the step where creative thinking kicks in. When you generate ideas, you have no rules except not to eliminate ideas that seem too far-fetched or odd. The goal for this step is to get a lot of ideas on paper, and the more ideas you can think of, the more likely you'll come up with a really creative solution that comes from "outside the box"—a phrase that describes ideas that aren't readily obvious.

When generating ideas, consider creating a list of possible ideas and role-playing (if you are able to work with another person) to get ideas flowing. This is a good time to take advantage of your strong or preferred learning style to stretch your imagination. For the "late for class" problem, you might identify some obvious solutions (such as riding your bike to class instead of driving), but by giving yourself room to be really creative and open, you might come up with some less-than-obvious ideas, such as packing your breakfast in a cooler and eating it *after* you find a parking spot—which doesn't fix the parking problem but helps resolve the overall problem of arriving late to class by saving you time each morning.

Step 3: Critically Evaluate Each Solution

To *critically evaluate* means that you consider the advantages and disadvantages, strengths and weaknesses, plusses and minuses of every option. Sometimes, it's helpful to construct a chart or table that lists each solution in one column, and then identifies the advantages, strengths, and plusses in the second column, and the disadvantages, weaknesses, and minuses in the third column. Forcing yourself to fill in every square in the grid ensures that you'll be thorough in considering both sides of a solution, especially if you find yourself preferring one particular solution from the very beginning.

The opinions of others can also be very helpful at this time. Your friends, parents, professors, and roommates can provide critical perspectives that may help you understand your options better than you can accomplish by yourself. For example, if you're considering the possibility of getting a part-time job to make the money you want to save for your ebook reader, your trusted advisors might help you discover some of the drawbacks of adding work to your weekly schedule because of their own personal experiences with similar circumstances.

Step 4: Select a Solution and Put It into Action

Some people tend to make decisions too quickly, before giving careful consideration to all the possible alternatives and potential outcomes. Other people, however, spend too much time considering all the alternatives and agonizing over possible outcomes, and they have trouble making a final decision.

The best course of action, of course, is to be somewhere in the middle: giving careful thought to each potential solution and then making a final decision in a timely manner. Once you've completed step 3 and you've carefully evaluated all of your possible solutions, you eventually need to make a decision.

Evaluate each possible solution based on its plusses and minuses, pick the one that has the most plusses, and then move on to put the solution into place. It's one thing to decide to do something, but it's something far different to put that decision into action. If you chose "riding your bike to class" as your solution to getting to class on time in the morning, then you need to have a bike with a lock and know where you can park it near your classroom. You might also need to make a test run on a day when you don't have class to figure out how long it will take to get from your dorm or apartment to your class using a different mode of transportation.

Analytical thinking can help you in classes that require you to learn processes.

Step 5: Evaluate the Solution

This is one of the easiest steps to overlook, yet it's also one of the most important. You can become a more effective problem solver and decision maker by revisiting the decisions you've made in the past and evaluating how they turned out in the long run. By examining several decisions over a six-month or one-year period, you'll see patterns, and if you practice the problem-solving process described here, you'll see a gradual, steady improvement in your decision making and problem solving over time.

By practicing this five-step process on a regular basis with relatively simple problems, you'll develop effective skills for tackling the really big problems when they arise. You'll also develop a lifelong habit that will serve you well.

INTEGRITY *Matters*

You can't be a true critical thinker without maintaining integrity in the process. To think critically with integrity, be fair in your judgments and represent others' views as accurately as possible. Critical thinkers know that every viewpoint has a counter-viewpoint that's equally valid, and critical thinkers with integrity acknowledge those other viewpoints without misrepresenting them.

Critical thinkers who have integrity also don't take shortcuts in the process of examining and judging an idea. The reward is the assurance that their final conclusions are fair.

YOUR TURN

In approximately 250 words, explain how you would handle the following situation: Your professor has asked you to write a paper on affirmative action in which you defend the practice, although you don't agree with this position.

THE UNWRITTEN RULES

Of Critical and Creative Thinking

■ **It won't always be obvious when you'll need to practice critical thinking.** You'll need to be an alert and careful information processor when you're in college, and almost every decision you face will require careful consideration. For example, during a meeting with your study group, one of your classmates might tell you that the exam will cover only the first five chapters of the textbook. You may not want to take one person's opinion at face value in this kind of situation, because the consequences will be significant if he or she is wrong. If you walk into class on exam day and discover that chapters 6 and 7 are also on the test, you'll have no one to blame but yourself.

■ **Too much stress, fatigue, and time pressure can kill creativity.** A little bit of stress might help to get you motivated, but too much of it will typically make you shut down. If you have a project or assignment that requires creative thinking, give yourself enough time to work on the project in advance. Some research suggests that your mind actually develops creative solutions when you're asleep, so give yourself a few days to generate ideas before the project deadline.

■ **Some of your best ideas will come when you least expect them.** Successful entrepreneurs and inventors often refer to thoughts that occur to them while they're in the shower or when they're engaged in an activity completely unrelated to the problem they're trying to solve. Keep a notepad and pencil handy wherever you are, so that you can put your ideas on paper when they occur. If you do, you'll reduce the chances of forgetting really good ideas when they come.

■ **Failing and making mistakes can help you become a better thinker.** Some students are so focused on getting perfect scores and all A's that they resist taking chances that might lead to failure. This approach might lead to having a high grade point average (GPA), but it will also stifle your ability to generate creative solutions. If you make mistakes or fail, review the circumstances and your decision-making process, and then use the experience to help you generate new ideas and solutions.

CASE SCENARIOS

1. Joan has been named a student ambassador for her college. One of her duties is to help prepare for fall orientation for new students. The program advisors have told the student ambassadors that last year, students had rated orientation poorly, because they had to wait in long lines to get registered and the information they received was too detailed and difficult to understand. Joan and her fellow ambassadors have been asked to create a new way of providing orientation to students. Joan has decided to use the feedback from last year's orientation to make improvements by addressing only what students said needed to be changed.

    Use the following scale to rate the decision that has been made (1 = Poor Decision, 5 = Excellent Decision). Be prepared to explain your answer.

    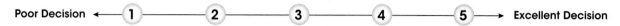

2. Sidra wants to earn money for college tuition next year, but she doesn't have the time to work 40 hours a week. Her creative-thinking process produces the following ideas: sell blood, tutor classmates, tattoo myself with a local company's logo and charge them for advertising, sell items on the Internet, work as a telemarketer, housesit for friends and family members. Sidra decides that selling blood once a month and working as a telemarketer for 35 hours a week are her best, most consistent options for earning money.

    Use the following scale to rate the decision that has been made (1 = Poor Decision, 5 = Excellent Decision). Be prepared to explain your answer.

    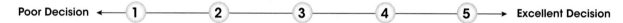

3. Kenya has decided to apply for a loan forgiveness program that will pay all her tuition as she completes a degree in computer networking. The loan forgiveness program requires that she find a job in networking within three months of graduation, or she will have to pay back the full amount of her loans. After she completes a year of her degree program, she learns that the job market for networking specialists doesn't look promising for the next five years. That might mean that she'll have great difficulty finding a job when she graduates in a year. Kenya decides to change majors and career paths, which means she'll be responsible for more than $20,000 in loans when she graduates. Her new career path, sales, has the potential for her to earn enough to pay back her loan over a few years if she works very hard and is successful in the job.

    Use the following scale to rate the decision that has been made (1 = Poor Decision, 5 = Excellent Decision). Be prepared to explain your answer.

Take It with You

Action Item	Deadline	First Step
Anticipate situations in which critical thinking will be needed.		
Develop effective creative-thinking skills and routines.		
Practice the five-step problem-solving process.		

REFERENCES

Diestler, S. (1998). *Becoming a critical thinker: A user friendly manual* (2nd ed.). Upper Saddle Creek River, NJ: Prentice Hall.

Harris, R. (2002). *Creative problem solving: A step-by-step approach*. Los Angeles: Pyrczak.

5 Learning Style Preference

JUANITA'S, MICHAEL'S, LAURA'S, AND EVAN'S STORIES

"Destination: Degree," the travel-themed majors fair for students who had not yet declared a major, was winding down after an afternoon of skits, presentations, and door prizes.

Jason, an orientation leader wearing an orange "Ask me!" T-shirt announced, "If everyone will score their inventories, I will explain how your learning style preference affects your study habits."

Michael, Laura, and Evan had asked Juanita to join them at the event, although she had already decided on a nursing major.

Evan finished scoring his inventory first. He told the others, "I am kinesthetic. That kind of makes sense. I teach kickboxing and learned how to do it by working out almost every day."

"I thought I would be kinesthetic, too," Michael said, rubbing his head, "but my preference is auditory. I guess it was all that time I spent in the military listening to orders."

"I am definitely an auditory learner, too," Laura told the group. "I got through all my classes in high school by listening to the lectures. I rarely took notes, because I liked to listen. Of course, it isn't working so well in my history class here in college."

Juanita chewed the eraser on her pencil before answering. "My learning preference is visual," she said. "I'm surprised! I thought that wanting to be a nurse would mean that I'm more of a kinesthetic learner."

"I don't think you have to worry about whether or not your career matches your learning style preference," said Michael. "I fixed machines in the military and was pretty good at it—and I'm an auditory learner."

"It still makes me wonder if I've chosen the right major," Juanita said. "Nursing is more than just memorizing pictures of the digestive system. What will I need to do when I start working on patients?"

"I think I would reconsider and choose something that matches what your preference is," suggested Laura. "Otherwise, you won't be successful."

"I guess I'll go talk to my advisor this afternoon," said Juanita.

Michael, Laura, Evan, and Juanita are learning how their personal learning style preferences are related to important issues in their lives, such as their career choices. Understanding your own learning style preference can be informative for your success, too. This chapter will help you to do the following:

- Describe different learning style preferences.
- Determine your learning style preferences.
- Use classroom and study strategies for different learning style preferences.
- Explore major and career options for different learning style preferences.

LEARNING OUTCOME

Recommend effective learning strategies for your learning style preference.

RECOGNIZE THE DIFFERENT TYPES OF INTELLIGENCE

Have you ever admired someone else's achievements and wished you could be that smart or talented? Do you think you have to be either "book smart" or athletic to be successful?

While you may think there are only one or two ways to be smart or talented, there are actually a number of ways that you can learn. Consider how you fit into the following categories of intelligence, which were developed by Harvard psychologist Howard Gardner (1999):

1. **Verbal/linguistic** intelligence is evident in people who can use language with ease. People who demonstrate verbal/linguistic intelligence enjoy reading and writing and may be journalists, novelists, playwrights, or comedians.
2. **Logical/mathematical** intelligence is demonstrated by ease and enjoyment with numbers and problems of logic. People who have strong logical/mathematical intelligence like to solve problems, find patterns, discover relationships between objects, and follow steps. Career choices for logical/mathematical people include science, computer technology, math, and engineering.
3. **Visual/spatial** intelligence is characterized by anything visual—paintings, photographs, maps, and architecture. People who have a strong visual/spatial sense are usually good at design, architecture, painting and sculpture, and map making.
4. **Bodily/kinesthetic** intelligence focuses on body movement. Bodily/kinesthetic people enjoy using their bodies to express themselves. Obvious career choices for people with this intelligence include dancing, sports, and dramatic arts.
5. **Musical/rhythmic** intelligence involves proficiency with the elements of music, such as rhythm, tone, tempo, and so on. People who have strong musical/rhythmic intelligence may use musical instruments or the human voice to express themselves. Career choices for someone with this intelligence include all types of musical performers.
6. **Interpersonal** intelligence is skill in relating with others. People with this skill read others' feelings well and act with others in mind.
7. **Intrapersonal** intelligence is centered on the ability to understand oneself. People who possess intrapersonal intelligence know how and why they do what they do.
8. **Naturalistic** intelligence involves enjoying and working well in an outdoor environment. Naturalistic people find peace in nature and enjoy having natural elements around them.

Reflect on the multiple intelligences by completing Activity 1.

ACTIVITY 1 Reflection on Multiple Intelligences

As you read about these various types of intelligence, which type or types describe you best? How could understanding this about yourself help you better succeed in college?

Different Theories Provide Unique Insights

There are numerous ways to see yourself and to understand your behavior in certain situations, and many education specialists and psychologists have created theories on how people take in and process information. They have also developed learning inventories and personality profiles to enhance your understanding of yourself. As you will discover, the learning process is somewhat complex, and involves more than just our preferences for how to create knowledge. In fact, many factors affect our ability to take in and process information.

Theories about the two hemispheres of the brain—known as the *left brain* and the *right brain*—have given us insight into how people think, learn, and see the world. People who have strong left-brain tendencies are likely to be logical, to see the parts rather than the whole, and to prefer to do activities step by step. They are also more analytical, realistic, and verbal than their right-brained companions. People who have strong right-brain tendencies tend to see the whole picture rather than the details, to work out of sequence, and to bring ideas together.

The Myers-Briggs Type Indicator (MBTI) is a personality assessment that provides information about how you prefer to think and act. For example, one dimension of the MBTI asks how outgoing, or extroverted, you are in certain situations, or how reserved, or introverted, you are. These questions indicate whether you are Extroverted (E) or Introverted (I). Both left-brain/right-brain inventories, or samples of the complete inventories, as well as the MBTI can be found in books or online.

Other inventories, such as the Dunn and Dunn Learning Styles Assessment and the PEPS Learning Styles Inventory, focus not only on how a person prefers to take in information but also on his or her social and environmental learning preferences. These types of inventories provide a thorough view of how you prefer to learn, including characteristics such as the temperature of the room, the amount of light and sound, and your preference for moving about as you learn.

Regardless of which learning theory or theories lead you to greater personal insight, by themselves, they are only partially helpful unless you use the information to benefit your situation. The purpose of a learning style inventory is to provide you with a basic understanding of the factors that affect your learning preferences, so that you can use this information to create an individualized and flexible learning plan for the various tasks and assignments that you will experience while in college. Ultimately, greater personal understanding and self-knowledge lead to action. Taking a learning style inventory can provide you not only with information about how you prefer to learn but also the roadmap for the journey to completing tasks and goals successfully.

It's in the SYLLABUS

Your professors' syllabi contain clues about how the content will address learning style preferences. For example, a syllabus for biology may include a description of a kinesthetic class project that will involve creating a three-dimensional model of DNA replication. Consider these questions:

- What learning styles will be addressed through the assignments in your classes this term?
- Which assignments do you think will be the most challenging for you to complete?
- Which assignments seem the most intriguing? Why?

Meeting EXPECTATIONS

The college will expect that I ...	To meet that expectation, I will ...
Example: . . . *learn the material that's presented to me, and earn good grades in the process.*	Example: . . . *find ways to translate material from my course work into my learning style preference.*

There are many ways of analyzing yourself and creating a plan of action for your work in college, but no single inventory, assessment, or work plan will completely reflect what an exceptional person you are and what unique circumstances you are in. No matter what inventory you take or what you learn about how you prefer to learn, don't view the results as the "final verdict" on your abilities and potential.

A LEARNING STYLE INVENTORY CAN HELP YOU DETERMINE YOUR LEARNING STYLE PREFERENCE

Knowing your learning style preference provides a foundation for understanding yourself in other aspects of your life. Information about what you like and dislike, how you relate to others, and how you can work productively will help you achieve your goals. As Lawrence (1995, p. 5) states in his book *People Types and Tiger Stripes,* knowing your learning style helps you make "dramatic improvements in the effectiveness of [your] work."

Among the many methods for measuring learning styles is the VAK Survey (Clark, 2004). Taking it will help you to understand yourself better and to identify which of the three different ways of receiving and learning new information is dominant for you. Your final score from this survey will give you some indication of whether you tend to receive and learn information best as a visual learner (by reading and writing or by seeing charts or other visual information), as an auditory learner (by hearing information or reading it out loud), or as a kinesthetic learner (by touching and moving).

VAK Survey

Read each statement carefully. To the left of each statement, write the number that best describes how each statement applies to you by using the following guide:

1	2	3	4	5
Almost never applies	Applies once in a while	Sometimes applies	Often applies	Almost always applies

INTEGRITY *Matters*

Understanding your learning style preference will provide helpful insights for use in developing effective study strategies in college. If you learn that a professor tends to favor a method of presenting information that's different than your own learning style preference, don't give up on the class or the professor. Learning how to work with people who are different from you is an important and valuable life skill.

YOUR TURN

In approximately 250 words, explain how you will identify your own learning style preference, how you will identify each professor's learning style preference, and how you will adapt to situations when you and your professor's styles don't match.

Answer honestly as there are no correct or incorrect answers. It is best if you do not think about each question too long, as this could lead you to the wrong conclusion.

Once you have completed all 36 statements (12 statements in three sections), total your score in the spaces provided.

Section 1—Visual

_____ 1. I take lots of written notes and/or draw mind maps.

_____ 2. When talking to someone else, I have a difficult time understanding those who do not maintain good eye contact with me.

_____ 3. I make lists and notes because I remember things better if I write them down.

_____ 4. When reading a novel, I pay a lot of attention to passages that describe the clothing, scenery, setting, etc.

_____ 5. I need to write down directions so that I can remember them.

_____ 6. I need to see the person I am talking to in order to keep my attention focused on the subject.

_____ 7. When meeting a person for the first time, I notice their style of dress, visual characteristics, and neatness first.

_____ 8. When I am at a party, one of the things I love to do is stand back and people-watch.

_____ 9. When recalling information, I can see it in my mind and remember where I saw it.

_____ 10. If I had to explain a new procedure or technique, I would prefer to write it out.

_____ 11. In my free time, I am most likely to watch television or read.

_____ 12. If my boss has a message for me, I am most comfortable when she sends a memo.

Total for Visual _____ (Note: The minimum is 12 and the maximum is 60.)

Section 2—Auditory

_____ 1. When I read, I read out loud or move my lips to hear the words in my head.

_____ 2. When talking to someone, I have a difficult time understanding those who do not talk or respond to me.

_____ 3. I do not take a lot of notes, but I still remember what was said. Taking notes often distracts me from the speaker.

_____ 4. When reading a novel, I pay a lot of attention to passages involving conversations, talking, speaking, dialogues, etc.

_____ 5. I like to talk to myself when solving a problem or writing.

_____ 6. I can understand what a speaker says, even if I am not focused on the speaker.

_____ 7. I remember things easier by repeating them over and over.

_____ 8. When I am at a party, one of the things I love to do is talk in-depth about a subject that is important to me with a good conversationalist.

_____ 9. I would rather receive information from the radio than read a newspaper.

_____ 10. If I had to explain a new procedure or technique, I would prefer telling about it.

_____ 11. With my free time, I am most likely to listen to music.

_____ 12. If my boss has a message for me, I am most comfortable when he or she calls me on the phone.

Total for Auditory _____ (Note: The minimum is 12 and the maximum is 60.)

Section 3—Kinesthetic

_____ 1. I am not good at reading or listening to directions. I would rather just start working on the task or project at hand.

_____ 2. When talking to someone, I have a difficult time understanding those who do not show any kind of emotional or physical support.

_____ 3. I take notes and doodle, but I rarely go back and look at them.

_____ 4. When reading a novel, I pay a lot of attention to passages revealing feelings, moods, action, drama, etc.

_____ 5. When I am reading, I move my lips.

_____ 6. I often exchange words, such as places or things, and use my hands a lot when I can't remember the right thing to say.

_____ 7. My desk appears disorganized.

_____ 8. When I am at a party, one of the things I love to do is enjoy the activities, such as dancing and games, and totally lose myself in the action.

_____ 9. I like to move around. I feel trapped when seated at a meeting or a desk.

_____ 10. If I had to explain a new procedure or technique, I would prefer actually demonstrating it.

_____ 11. With my free time, I am most likely to exercise.

_____ 12. If my boss has a message for me, I am most comfortable when she talks to me in person.

Total for Kinesthetic _____ (Note: The minimum is 12 and the maximum is 60.)

Kinesthetic learning involves using your hands and body to master a concept.

Scoring Procedure

Total each section, and write the sum in the corresponding block below:

Visual	Auditory	Kinesthetic
Number of points:	Number of points:	Number of points:

While you prefer to learn using the method with the highest score, you will normally learn best by using all three styles, not just your preferred learning style.

YOUR CLASSROOM AND STUDY TACTICS CAN REFLECT YOUR LEARNING STYLE PREFERENCE

Note taking is an essential part of the college experience, whether it is taking notes while listening to a lecture or while reading to prepare for class. How you decide to take notes may very well depend on how you prefer to take in information and learn. The following strategies are intended for those who have visual, auditory, kinesthetic, or a combination of learning style preferences.

Visual Learners

Visual learners often prefer to receive visual information when listening to a lecture. Visuals can include presentation slides, a video, or props that are used for demonstration. If none of these is used, visual learners may want to create their own visual representations in their notes.

Take, for example, a lecture on academic integrity. An instructor may talk through or write down a few key ideas on the board or in handouts that look like this:

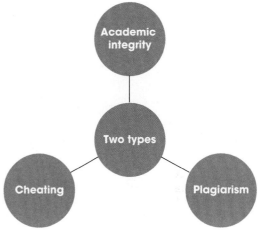

> ****Academic Integrity—doing what is right academically, even in the face of adversity.

> *Two kinds of violations of academic integrity include cheating and plagiarism.

> Plagiarism comes in several forms, but the two most common are no documentation and cut-and-paste. Other forms are also self-plagiarism, following too close to original, word-for-word, and buying papers...

A visual learner may take this information and create a visual representation of the definitions and types that looks like this:

Auditory Learners

For auditory learners, it may be tempting only to listen, rather than to also write down the general idea of what's being said. However, taking notes will be essential to recalling the information later. Recording lectures—with permission from the professor—may benefit auditory learners.

Kinesthetic Learners

The act of taking notes by writing or typing them provides kinesthetic learners with a physical activity that makes it easier to remember what they have written. Kinesthetic learners can benefit from using physical activity or objects when they review their notes shortly after taking them. For example, if you are using formulas to calculate volume in your math class, you may want to review your notes by creating your own volume problems and solutions with common household items. The act of pouring and measuring water and then calculating your measurements will make it easier to remember the process when you complete homework problems or take a test.

CHOOSE A STUDY STRATEGY THAT ENHANCES YOUR LEARNING STYLE PREFERENCE

Just as note taking in the way that suits your learning style preference will help you take more meaningful notes, you will study better for your courses by using strategies that enhance your learning style. Visual learners, for example, may benefit from reading through notes and reviewing images that represent the material. These images may be textbook illustrations or diagrams presented during a lecture, or learners may create images when they take notes (for example, mind maps).

Take into account your learning style preference when you are making a study plan.

Mind maps are visual representations of information that show the connections among the pieces of information. While there is a basic structure for a mind map, learners can customize a visual image with colors and symbols that make the most sense to them. The key to creating a mind map is to connect the information in meaningful ways to show the relationships among the pieces of information. Exhibit 1 shows an example of a mind map. Other study strategies for visual learners can include reviewing videos of the concepts or processes that are part of the course.

Study strategies for auditory learners can include reading notes aloud or talking through the concepts. Auditory learners can use a recording device and play back the recording or participate in a study group and take turns talking through the content and listening. Video or audio files may also be available as part of the course content that can be used to supplement studying.

Kinesthetic learners may want to include practice questions in their studying. For math courses, kinesthetic learners may want to work through practice problems. For any course that requires a short discussion or essay, they may want to practice writing

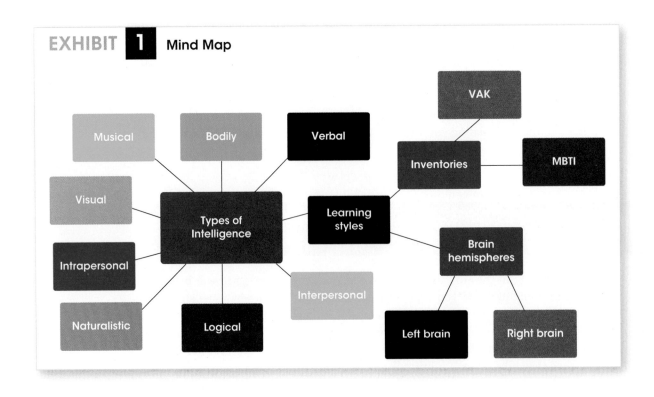

EXHIBIT 1 Mind Map

THE UNWRITTEN RULES

Of Learning Style Preference

■ **Your professors will tend to present information in class that favors *their* learning preference.** If you learn that you're a kinesthetic learner, don't expect your professor to provide course information or design class activities that accommodate your preference. Instead, you'll need to study materials from the course on your own in a way that helps you the most.

■ **Emerging technologies are making it easier to accommodate your learning style preferences.** For example, the growing popularity of educational content in video form, such as the instructional videos from the Khan Academy (www.khanacademy.org), can help learners who favor visual information more than written text, as can the presentation tool called Prezi, which is emerging as an alternative to Powerpoint. The growing use of audio podcasts and iTunesU to accompany class lectures is another example of technology's support of learning style differences.

■ **It's best not to define yourself by a single learning preference.** As you take the various inventories and tests that are mentioned in this chapter or elsewhere, don't just look for your dominant learning style preference. Note also what your secondary preferences are. Your success as a learner will require you to draw upon a variety of learning preferences depending on the type of content and the professor's expectations. In fact, if you discover that your visual/spatial learning style is your second or third most preferred style, you may want to stretch yourself in college to use visual depictions of concepts whenever possible to develop and refine that style of thinking.

responses and creating outlines for longer essays. A good way for a kinesthetic learner to study for an art class, for example, or any class that uses visual images is to re-create with paper and colored pencils the artwork he or she is studying. There's no need to strive for masterpiece quality when re-creating works of art! The physical activity of drawing the wavy lines in the background of Edvard Munch's painting *The Scream* will help you recall the piece on an exam.

USE YOUR LEARNING PREFERENCES TO EXPLORE MAJOR AND CAREER OPTIONS

Discovering your learning style preference and your personality type can help you set realistic short-term and long-term goals. For example, confirming that you have a visual learning preference and that you work well with deadlines and can stay organized may help you realize that your long-term goal of being a designer is a good fit for you. However, identifying your style and type should not limit your choices or keep you from working on areas of your learning style and personality that may be weak or get less attention.

If you're a strong visual learner but are taking a class that relies on listening effectively and critically, you should use that opportunity to become a better listener and to improve your auditory learning style by following tips for effective listening. If you work better alone and have a strong kinesthetic learning style preference, choosing a career as a computer technician may play to your strengths, but you may also find yourself working with others collaboratively and communicating frequently in writing and verbally. See Exhibit 2 for examples of careers and majors and how they connect to learning style preferences.

Your learning style preference may also influence your career choice.

One way to see the relationship between learning style preferences and career choices is to ask people who are successful in their careers about their own learning style preferences. Look for both patterns and exceptions. For example, do people who excel in accounting tend to favor one style of learning over others? What about successful architects? Identifying patterns can be informative but shouldn't discourage or restrict your own decisions. For example, if you favor a kinesthetic learning style but have a strong interest in a career in graphic design, look for ways to take advantage of your distinctive style to develop new and creative methods for developing visual depictions of concepts and information.

Whatever your learning style and personality preferences are, consider how other styles and types will factor into your short-term and long-term educational goals. Then look for opportunities to strengthen the less-developed sides of your learning style and personality. Work on becoming more comfortable in a variety of situations and being a well-rounded person.

EXHIBIT 2 — Learning Style Preferences, College Majors, and Careers

Learning Style Preference	College Majors	Careers
Visual	Art, graphic design, architecture, video production	Art teacher, artist, graphic designer, architect, interior designer, video producer
Auditory	Music, communications, counseling	Musician, music educator, marketing director, public relations director, counselor
Kinesthetic	Sciences, sociology, computer technology, culinary arts, theater	Nurse, doctor, therapist, networking specialist, computer technician, actor, director

CASE SCENARIOS

1. Katie is a multimodal learner, which means she has no strong learning preference. All of her classes have a heavy reading load, and two classes—Introduction to Drawing and Biology with Lab—involve hands-on work. She has decided to study with a friend of hers whose learning style preference is aural. Katie and her friend decide that the best way to study for their classes is to record lectures, talk about what they are learning in class, and read their textbooks aloud.

   Use the following scale to rate the decision that has been made (1 = Poor Decision, 5 = Excellent Decision). Be prepared to explain your answer.

2. Isaac has a music background because of his participation in the church choir, and there is rarely a day that music isn't a part of his life. He took a learning style inventory and was surprised that his learning preference is visual. In fact, he scored very low on the aural preference questions. In the past, he would listen to music or watch television while studying, but he has now decided that he should not have any distractions while studying. He has also decided to create diagrams with his notes so that they are more visually appealing, and to use visualization techniques when trying to remember information from his class.

   Use the following scale to rate the decision that has been made (1 = Poor Decision, 5 = Excellent Decision). Be prepared to explain your answer.

3. Horatio took a learning style inventory and found out that he is a kinesthetic learner, prefers mornings, and works best in groups. He has registered for a visual art appreciation class in the late afternoon. He really needs this class, and it was offered only at this time. So far, Horatio has enjoyed the class, especially the historical parts, but he's having a hard time taking notes and keeping up with all the different artists, styles, and media, because his professor lectures while showing slides of works of art. One group project will require Horatio to work with others to present the works and themes of a selected artist from the twenty-first century. Horatio doesn't feel that this class really connects with his learning style preference and isn't sure what to do to get a better grasp on the concepts. So he's decided to focus on his other classes, which are more rewarding and better match his learning style preference. He decides that not every class will be an opportunity to do his best.

   Use the following scale to rate the decision that has been made (1 = Poor Decision, 5 = Excellent Decision). Be prepared to explain your answer.

Take It with You

Action Item	Deadline	First Step
Determine your learning style preference.	_____	_____
		_____
Create one study strategy based on your learning style preference.	_____	_____
		_____
		_____
Explore a major, degree, or career that connects to your learning style preference.	_____	_____
		_____
		_____
_____	_____	_____
_____		_____

REFERENCES

Clark, D. R. (2004). *The art and science of leadership*. Retrieved from http://nwlink .com/~donclark/leader/leader.html

Gardner, H. (1999). *Intelligence reframed: Multiple intelligences for the 21st century*. New York: Basic Books.

Lawrence, G. (1995). *People types and tiger stripes* (3rd ed.). Gainesville, FL: CAPT.

6 Listening and Note Taking

Laura settled into her seat in the front row of her world civilization class. Class was about to start.

The professor began, explaining to students, "The clip we are about to watch discusses the ancient library in Timbuktu."

"I would much rather watch these videos than listen to Professor Reynolds talk," a classmate named Jamie whispered to Laura, causing her to miss the professor's explanation of the video.

"Hey? Do you have an extra pen?" Jamie asked, loud enough to be heard over the video. Laura handed Jamie a pen and made a note to fill in the gaps in her notes that resulted from being distracted.

After the video had ended, Laura's professor provided the information she had been waiting for. He said, "You have the material that was assigned for reading, the information I cover in the lecture, and then anything else that I bring in. All of this should be studied for the test."

"And he will put *everything* on the test," thought Laura.

Even with help from her mentor and the tutor in the learning assistance center, Laura had her work cut out for her. The book was arranged chronologically, but her professor lectured on causes and effects in history. Her notes seemed like a jumbled mess. Then, there were the tests that covered major themes, such as important reformers and federal policies. Laura struggled in this class to find the right note-taking method to accommodate all the different types of information.

As Laura headed out of class, her talkative classmate, Jamie, stopped her. He asked, "Do you want to share notes and study together? I don't have much written down, and I noticed you take good notes."

Laura didn't have much time to think about whether it would be helpful to study with someone who seemed so disorganized and inattentive, but she knew she would need help, too.

"Sure," she told Jamie before heading to her next class. "Bring your notes and book, and meet me in the library."

Like Laura, your success in college will depend in part on your ability to listen well and record what you've heard in class in your notes. To help you succeed in this effort, this chapter will help you do the following:

- Prepare for class.
- Practice active and critical listening.
- Effectively record and organize your in-class notes.

LEARNING OUTCOME

Create class notes using active listening techniques.

SUCCESS IN CLASS BEGINS WITH PREPARATION

Preparing to listen and staying focused will make listening—and remembering what was said—more effective.

In college, as in life, preparation is one of the keys to success. Much of your academic success will be determined by how well you prepare for your classes before they even begin. Just as you would invest time and effort to prepare for a first date, a job interview, or a meeting with a high-level executive, so you should prepare for a class before you walk into the classroom.

Because a great deal of information is typically shared during class, preparing effectively will be particularly important in helping you to listen well, to organize what you hear with effective notes, and to remember and recall the information later when you need it for projects and exams and your career. Here are a number of guidelines for ways to prepare effectively for class:

- *Read and study preassigned materials.* Your professor will often provide a syllabus that tells you what chapters or other written content is assigned for each day of class. If you take time to read the assigned materials before class, not only will you be more familiar with the content to be discussed in class, but you will also be able to learn more effectively and, in the long run, spend less time later preparing for quizzes and exams. Your professor might even provide a copy of the lecture notes in advance via the course website. If so, print out the notes and bring them to class. When you build your schedule for the term, include time for reading course materials before class. If you step into a class and have already read the assigned materials, you will better understand what the professor is talking about, you will be familiar with the terminology and concepts, and you will have good questions to ask in class for clarification and further learning. This will help you take notes more effectively and will enhance your class participation effectiveness, because you will be better equipped to actively participate in class discussions.

- *Minimize out-of-class distractions.* At times during your college experience, you may have to work late, stay up all night with a sick child, or help a friend who has just had a crisis. If not handled well, these stressful experiences might affect your performance in class. As much as possible, leave your personal life at the door and concentrate on the class that you are sitting in. How?

  - Put time into your schedule, outside class time, to address personal matters.
  - *Turn off* your cell phone while in class. Don't just set it to vibrate.
  - Build in 5 to 10 minutes before every class to clear your mind of personal issues and other distractions and to transition your mind to prepare for the class at hand. Reviewing the assigned readings or your notes from last class can aid in this process.

EXHIBIT 1

Tip	Explanation	Example
Prepare ahead of time.	Read all pages from textbooks, handouts, and extra material that your professor assigns or mentions.	Before the lecture on the American Dream in Arthur Miller's *Death of a Salesman*, read the entire play.
Minimize in-class distractions.	Make sure that you have few, if any, items or people near you that can get your attention.	Turn your phone to silent mode and stow it in your backpack before walking into class.
Maintain a positive attitude.	Stay positive about a class no matter what others have said negatively about it or what you have experienced so far.	On your way to class, think about five positive aspects of the class that will help you achieve your ultimate academic or career goal.
Minimize out-of-class distractions.	Your situation and thoughts can get in the way of concentrating on what is being said. Work to focus on the present, not the past or the future.	If there is something on your mind, write down your concerns before going to class and promise yourself to think about it after class is over.
Prepare physically.	Take care of yourself by getting enough rest and food or drink before you go to class. Wear appropriate clothing so that you will be comfortable.	Grab your jacket, an energy bar, and a bottle of water before you go to your classes.

- *Prepare for class psychologically by preparing physically.* Make sure you have eaten something before each class, so that you won't be distracted by a growling stomach. Moreover, dress in layers in case the room is an uncomfortable temperature. Nothing is more distracting than being too hot or too cold. Getting plenty of sleep the night before class will also help you pay attention and listen effectively. Although adequate sleep may be a luxury if you work a late shift or if you get up in the middle of the night to take care of a child, be sure you make an effort to get a good night's sleep as often as possible. You won't be able to maintain high concentration and retention or even good health without adequate rest.

Review Exhibit 1, which provides tips for preparing to listen.

ACTIVITY 1

Which of the following will be most challenging for you when you prepare for class: preparing physically, reducing out-of-class distractions, or completing assigned readings before class?

EFFECTIVE LISTENING IS BOTH ACTIVE AND CRITICAL

Active listening is a term that you may hear in college classes. Someone who listens actively is concentrating on what is being said and taking steps to remember the information. To be an active listener, you must decide that listening is a worthwhile activity and that important information is being shared.

Follow these tips to listen actively and effectively:

- Write down important facts, concepts, and terms in notebooks designated for specific courses.
- Use visual tools (charts, tables, arrows, numbers) to organize content in notes.
- Raise your hand and ask questions to clarify content or to resolve confusing concepts.
- Maintain an upright posture in the chair to keep your body in an alert position.
- Create acronyms and use other mnemonic devices to help organize and remember information.
- Write down questions, feelings, opinions, and other reactions in the margins of your notes for later review and consideration.
- Maintain a positive attitude about each class. Look for connections between content discussed in the class, your other classes, and your future career. Consider the possibility that at any moment, you could learn something new—something that you never knew before. That's an exciting prospect that can keep you engaged in the class, no matter what the topic or how it's being discussed.
- Avoid in-class distractions.

   1. Clear your desk of everything except your textbook, a pen, and paper. Stow other items in your backpack or underneath your desk or table.
   2. If you need to get anything out of your backpack during class (such as a dictionary), minimize the disruption by being as quiet as possible.
   3. If you find yourself next to a chatty classmate or one who likes to write notes to you, simply move. Even if you are politely listening to this person or reading his or her messages, you will be guilty of disrupting the class by association. Talkative classmates make it difficult for you and others to listen, and they distract you from taking good notes.

To Listen Critically Is to Listen Well

As stated earlier, active listening, much like active reading, involves focusing on the task at hand and concentrating on what's being conveyed. Another part of listening effectively is listening critically—or processing what you have heard and evaluating it. Listening critically will help you make decisions about what is important and what isn't

Meeting EXPECTATIONS

The college will expect that I ...	To meet that expectation, I will ...
Example: ... *minimize listening barriers when I'm in class.*	Example: ... *I'll store my cell phone in my backpack to keep me from being distracted, and I'll sit at the front of the classroom.*

important, what is objective and what is biased, and what should be stored for later and what should be discarded.

Listening critically is a skill that you should practice regularly. Your college professors will invite you to think critically and will challenge your assumptions at times. This may feel uncomfortable, but you'll recall from elsewhere in this book that critical thinking is a key part of learning. As you get more comfortable with listening actively and critically, you'll move from merely listening and taking notes that reflect what your instructors have said to listening to evaluate and ask questions of the notes you have taken.

Here are some questions to consider as you work on listening critically:

It's in the SYLLABUS

By looking at your syllabus, determine how the information will be presented in a given course: Will it be presented by chapters, topics, or units? Also consider these questions:

- What are the note-taking expectations for the class?

- Is that information in the syllabus, or did you learn it from your professor or other students?

- *Speaker.* Is the speaker a credible source? How do I know? What possible biases does he or she have? What is his or her experience with the topic?
- *Message.* What is the speaker's purpose? What details does he or she use to convey the message?
- *Details.* Is the speaker using facts or opinions? How do I know? Which type of details work best for what the speaker is trying to convey?
- *Self-knowledge.* What do I already know about the topic? How does what the speaker is saying conflict or support my beliefs and opinions? Do I feel I have learned something new?
- *Larger picture.* How does what the speaker is saying fit into the larger picture? How can I relate his or her message to something I already know about life or the world at large? Are there any connections between what I have heard and what I have experienced?

Answering some of these questions will get you started on the right path to listening critically. Even though you will be listening critically and mentally asking questions of what you are hearing, you will still need to "tune in," rather than "tune out," when you hear something that you don't agree with or don't understand.

Remember, too, that *critical* does not mean *negative*. If you find that what you are hearing doesn't hold up to what you know about the subject or that the speaker isn't credible, ask questions that are respectful and curious. Most speakers don't mind being politely challenged or debated.

TAKING NOTES IS PART OF THE LISTENING PROCESS

There are numerous methods of taking notes for class. Your goal should be to find the note-taking strategy that works best for you.

Remember that you may have to adapt your note-taking style to each course, including each professor's teaching style, and to your own learning style preference. For example, outlining may work well in a history course in which the instructor writes key terms on the board and organizes the lecture around these key ideas. But if your professor prefers unstructured discussion, you'll need to adapt your note-taking strategy to make the most of disorganized information.

INTEGRITY *Matters*

There are websites where college students from across the country post their notes from various courses. It's tempting to download notes from these sites, rather than write your own. Some professors consider using other students' notes a form of plagiarism and a violation of their intellectual property rights. Also keep in mind the benefit of taking notes yourself: It helps you learn and remember the information better. If you simply copy someone else's notes, you won't get that benefit anymore.

YOUR TURN

In approximately 250 words, explain how you feel about using other students' notes from your classes instead of or in addition to your own.

Whatever you choose for the particular course, your learning style preference, and the specific situation, remember these tips when taking notes:

- *Listen for the main ideas.* Professors will slow down and emphasize details, terms, and definitions. They may even use verbal signposts, such as "The most important thing to remember is . . ." "This may appear on an exam," and "Two crucial points about . . ." If the instructor writes or hands out an outline, you can be sure that it contains the main points of the lecture.
- *Leave plenty of "white space" (blank areas on the paper) when taking notes.* Don't try to fill your page with as much information as possible. You will need the white space to add more notes or to connect ideas once you have reviewed them.
- *Review your notes as soon as possible after class.* Waiting for two weeks to review your notes will ensure that you won't remember everything that you have written or how it all fits together. Most experts suggest reviewing notes within two days of a class.

Knowing How Information Is Presented Can Improve Your Note Taking

Learning to listen effectively is the first step to taking good notes, but you'll also benefit from understanding how information can be presented during a lecture. As you attend more classes, you'll probably notice that professors have certain ways in which they present their materials. Some follow the textbook, presenting information in the same order. Others lecture only on new material that can't be found in the textbook or other course materials. Others use a combination of the two methods. Reading assigned chapters and other materials before class will allow you to determine which information in the lecture is new and which has been covered in the assigned reading materials.

Here are some of the different ways that course materials might be organized:

- *Chronological:* Details are arranged in time (first this happened, then this happened, etc.).

Example of Chronological Lecture Notes

> 1801: United Kingdom of Great Britain is created.
>
> 1803: Louisiana Purchase is made by Thomas Jefferson.
>
> 1815: Battle of Waterloo signals end of Napoleon's career.

- *Cause/Effect:* Details are arranged by presenting a cause and then its effects, or an effect and then its causes.

Example of Cause/Effect Lecture Notes

> Cause: Civil War
>
> Effects: slavery ended, industrialism began, nation brought back together, federal government proved stronger than states

- *Compare/Contrast:* Details are arranged by similarities and differences.

Example of Compare/Contrast Lecture Notes

> Similarities between Robert Frost and Walt Whitman: they were males; they used nature in their poetry; and they were considered "poets of the people."
>
> Differences between Frost and Whitman: Frost's poetry is more structured, while Whitman's is more open and loose; Whitman's speakers are more positive and upbeat than Frost's; Whitman lived during the 19th century, while Frost lived in both the 19th and 20th centuries.

- *Most important/Least important:* Details are arranged in order of importance. The most important detail can come first, with minor supporting details to follow, or the least important details can start a list, with a major detail to follow.

Example of Most Important/Least Important Lecture Notes

> **Truman Commission (1946)***
>
> Barriers to equal opportunity & toward equalizing opportunity (most important sections in the doc.)
>
> Number who should receive higher education & the role of education (2nd most import.)
>
> The need for general education & a time of crisis (least import. secs.)
>
> *first pres. comm. on hi. ed.

THE UNWRITTEN RULES

Of Listening and Note Taking

- **The ability to listen well is arguably more critical to your success than your ability to speak well.** Why else would you have two ears but only one mouth?

- **By preparing for class, listening well, and taking good notes, you can actually reduce your study time.** Professors will hesitate to suggest this, because they don't want students to reduce how much time they devote to studying. But the fact is that if you listen to, process, and organize information effectively the first time, you won't take as long to review and remember the same information the second time.

- **Sitting next to your friends or students you know in class might not be the best idea.** The probability of being distracted increases when you are close to people you know. It might be socially awkward to tell friends that you're not going to sit next to them in class, but your academic performance will stand to gain from making wise choices.

Taking good notes is an important part of the learning process.

Note-Taking Strategies: Pick What Works Best for You

Once you understand how each of your professors tends to present information or how the information is structured in your course materials, you can develop your own strategy for organizing your notes. Here are some strategies that you can try for yourself.

Outlining

Using an outline is a good method for taking notes if the instructor is organized and offers information in a logical pattern. Some instructors encourage outlining by writing key words and concepts on the board or an overhead projecting device. If your instructor organizes lectures or class discussions in this manner, you'll be able to write an outline for your notes quite easily. The key to making an outline effective is to provide plenty of space between items so you can fill in the blank spaces with extra information.

The T-System

Cornell University professor Walter Pauk (2004) developed a system for note taking that has been popular with many students. The *Cornell system*, also known as the *T-system*, is ideal for learners who benefit from the visual impact of organized notes, and it can benefit other types of learners, such as Laura, because it is an organized way to take and review notes.

The key to the Cornell system is to divide your notebook paper before you begin writing. To do so, draw a horizontal line across a piece of paper 2 inches from the bottom of the page. Then draw a vertical line from the horizontal line to the top of the page about 2 inches from the left-hand margin. The page should look like Exhibit 2.

The largest area, the right-hand column, is used for taking notes during a lecture. The left-hand column is used for writing down questions while taking notes in case there is material you don't understand or there are possible exam questions that you think about as you are writing. The final section, at the bottom, is reserved for summarizing your notes as you review them. The act of summarizing should help you understand and remember the information.

Adapting Your Notes for Different Disciplines

Learn how to adapt your note-taking format or style for different classes and subjects:

- *Art:* In an art appreciation class, you'll need to identify eras (twentieth century), movements (Cubism), and artists (Picasso), as well as their characteristics, as seen in drawings, paintings, and sculptures. Quickly sketching the works in your notes and listing the characteristic details will help you record the information you are

EXHIBIT

Add questions or important notes here. | Write notes here.

Add summary of notes here after you read through them.

receiving through lectures. You may also notice that in the study of art, there are times of intense change (usually coinciding with a world or cultural event), followed by periods in which artists imitate or slightly modify the new styles. As you review your notes, look for patterns within groups of artworks and for points of contrast.

- *Music:* In a music appreciation class, follow the same note-taking suggestions as for an art appreciation class. But instead of re-creating a painting or sculpture in your notes, write down descriptions of what you hear and what the sounds remind you of: Are the sounds fast or slow? Do you hear one instrument or many? Does it sound like a stampede or a trip down a lazy river? "Translating" music samples into written notes, as well as reviewing music clips on your own, will strengthen your understanding of the material. As with your art notes, when you review, look for patterns across movements and eras and identify contrasting ideas and elements.

- *Literature:* Taking notes in a literature class will require you to complete the assigned readings before class and to have annotated and highlighted your text. Because literature classes, even survey classes, focus more on discussion than on lecture, you'll want to be prepared to take notes on the analysis. As with music and art classes, being familiar with basic terminology before you get to class will help you take better notes. As you review your notes, look for ideas that pull the different readings together.

- *Languages:* Foreign language classes center more on speaking and interacting than on listening to lectures. Taking notes will not necessarily be advantageous, for you'll need to focus all your attention on listening actively, processing what you hear, and then interacting. Daily preparation is essential to learning a foreign language. Take notes as you encounter new material, and ask questions in class to clarify anything you don't understand. Be sure to review any notes that you do take soon after the class. As you review your notes, categorize content, such as "Irregular verbs," and include any tips for using or remembering the parts of speech.

- *Science:* Learning concepts and processes is key in science classes, and your notes should reflect that. Prepare for class by reading assigned materials, making note of new vocabulary words, and studying diagrams and figures in the textbook and handouts. As with any class, ask questions if you're having trouble following the steps of a process. As you review your notes, consider the different ways that you can represent these concepts and processes visually and physically to help you remember them better.

- *History:* History class lectures are usually presented in chronological order, so using the tips provided earlier for information that follows a time sequence will help you take notes in these classes. However, you will also be required to move beyond specific dates and events by considering overall themes, ideas, and movements. In addition to chronological order, cause/effect organization may be used in lectures, in which you list and elaborate on the effects of a cause or the causes of an effect. An example of a cause/effect lecture topic in a history class is "The economic and social effects of the end of the Civil War." As you review your notes, look for major themes and try to recall actions that led to important events.

Your note-taking strategy may differ depending on the course you are taking.

- *Math:* Taking good notes in your math classes will require you to prepare for and attend each class meeting. As with studying a foreign language, studying for math should be an everyday occurrence, because the skills you learn in each class build on the skills you learned in the class before. When reviewing your notes, recopy them and make sure that you understand, line by line, each problem that you copy. If you have any questions, write them in the margins of your notes and ask questions during the next class meeting.

| ACTIVITY 2 | Complete the Following Table Based on the Courses You Are Taking This Semester | |

Course	Typical Presentation of Information by Instructor	Method for Taking Notes

By preparing in advance for class, listening both actively and critically, and taking effective notes, you can greatly enhance your college success.

CASE SCENARIOS

1. Juan is taking a visual arts class and having trouble making sense of his notes each week, because they contain information that pertains to specific works of art. The instructor doesn't hand out reproductions of the art, so students must sketch the pieces during class, which takes most of them a long time. Juan has difficulty sketching and writing quickly, so he decides that it would be best just to listen while the professor lectures. Juan plans to print out copies of the artworks from the Internet and make notes on the copies at home.

   Use the following scale to rate the decision that has been made (1 = Poor Decision, 5 = Excellent Decision). Be prepared to explain your answer.

2. Theo borrowed Jon's notes for his College Algebra class and promised to return them before the next exam. Unfortunately, Theo has lost the notes, and with only two days left before the exam, he isn't sure what to do. Jon is a good student and probably doesn't need the notes as much as Theo does, but Theo wants to be able to borrow notes from Jon in the future. Theo decides to borrow another classmate's notes, copy them, and then give the copies to Jon after explaining what happened.

   Use the following scale to rate the decision that has been made (1 = Poor Decision, 5 = Excellent Decision). Be prepared to explain your answer.

   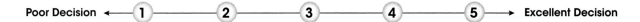

3. Karla has a learning disability, and she struggles with taking notes. Her counselor has assigned her a note-taker. Now that Karla is getting help with writing down notes, she has stopped preparing for class and stopped listening closely. But sometimes, she doesn't get the notes from her note-taker until a week later. Instead of complaining to her counselor, Karla decides to ask another classmate if she can borrow his notes each week.

   Use the following scale to rate the decision that has been made (1 = Poor Decision, 5 = Excellent Decision). Be prepared to explain your answer.

Take It with You

Action Item	Deadline	First Step
Develop a plan of action for preparing for each class.	_____	
Develop an active listening plan, and gather the necessary notebooks and other supplies for doing so.	_____	
Practice critical listening in every class.	_____	
Practice different note-taking strategies to learn which ones work best in different situations.	_____	
_____	_____	

REFERENCE

Pauk, W., & Owens, J.R. (2004). *How to study in college*. Boston, MA: Cengage.

7 Reading and Note Taking

Evan sighed deeply after finishing his weekly list of assigned reading:

To Do This Week
- Biology: pages 54–108
- Aviation: pages 72–144
- Autobiography: pages 1–213

Even though he could bench-press hundreds of pounds, Evan felt weak when he thought about reading. He had discovered early on that college without reading was like kickboxing without sore muscles.

When Evan ran into Michael in the hall after class last week, he complained about what he had to do and why he didn't want to do it.

Michael told him, "Evan, I know exactly what you need to do. I just got help with my algebra homework, and the tutor explained it in a way that I could get it."

"It's not that I don't know what to do," Evan replied. "I just don't like to read. It's boring."

Michael laughed. "It does seem boring at first," he agreed, "but you'll get better at reading the more you do it."

"I don't think I want to get that good at it," Evan joked.

Despite his joking, Evan went to the only place he knew he could get help: the college tutoring center.

Like Evan, you will be expected to do a lot of assigned reading in college. To support your success with this challenge, this chapter will help you do the following:

- Become an active and critical reader.
- Take good notes while reading.
- Combine class and text notes.

LEARNING OUTCOME

Create reading notes using active and critical reading.

 (www.mystudentsuccesslab.com) is an online solution designed to help you 'Start strong, Finish stronger' by building skills for ongoing personal and professional development.

READING IS AN ACTIVE PROCESS

Reading actively includes being focused on what you are reading.

It's in the SYLLABUS

Review your syllabi and determine how many pages (approximately) you are required to read each week for *all* your classes combined. Also consider these questions:

- Do some classes require more reading than others? If so, which ones?

- Are some of the reading assignments harder than others? If so, which ones?

- How do you plan to handle the reading load this semester?

- Do you expect to keep up with the reading? Why or why not?

Reading is important to your college education, as well as your career and personal success, for several reasons: It helps you develop knowledge about a range of subjects; it improves your understanding of others and the world around you; and it helps you understand yourself, which will assist you in making better life choices.

What do you picture in your mind when someone tells you that he or she has been reading for three hours? Perhaps you envision the person reclining in a comfortable chair with a cup of coffee. Although this may be an enjoyable way to read, the reality is that a lot of us would probably fall asleep if we sat in that position for any length of time! When you read books, articles, and online content to learn and study, you'll have a lot more success if you make reading a far more active process.

Active reading is a term that you may hear often in college, along with *active listening*. It means that you are fully engaged in reading by focusing your mind and body on the activity. Many first-time students read passively, rather than actively, and don't fully concentrate on the materials. Just reading the words isn't enough for college classes. Instead, you must be a part of the process by making sure you comprehend what you are reading.

Critical reading is another term that you'll hear frequently in college. Some students think that critical reading means having a negative reaction to what they have read. Actually, critical reading involves a series of steps to react and respond to the reading—either positively or negatively, depending on the materials. The goal of critical reading is to question and evaluate information, not to take it at face value.

Critical reading and active reading both require developing a set of skills, which will take practice. The following sections provide specific strategies for developing and practicing these skills.

Successful Reading Begins with Preparation

Most of your reading assignments in college will be assigned by your instructors. You'll be given handouts, syllabi, and chapters to read in your textbooks. How do you manage it all without getting behind and overwhelmed at the start of the semester?

Preparation is the key. Follow these guidelines to help you successfully prepare for effective reading:

- *Assume all assigned materials are important.* When your professors assign content for you to read, they do so after carefully evaluating a large volume of materials. Take advantage of the fact that they've worked hard to pick the right content for you to read.

- *Organize reading materials according to their lengths and due dates.* Begin reading the most important or urgent assignments first, and then work your way through the rest of the content.

- *Mark a specific time and place to read on your calendar, preferably at the same time each day.* Doing this will help your mind and body to prepare for the reading task.

- *Find a comfortable, quiet area to read.* Reading in the right environment will help you focus on what you're reading.

- *Establish routine breaks from reading.* Get up, walk around, get a drink of water, and get the circulation going in your legs again. Taking breaks in which you physically move around the room will help improve your concentration and keep you from falling asleep.

- *Establish a clear purpose for reading.* For example, if you know your purpose is to understand how food passes through the body's digestive system, then when you sit down with the textbook for your anatomy class, you will be in the right frame of mind.

- *Take good care of your body and mind throughout the term.* You won't be able to read effectively if you are tired, hungry, or sick. Don't try to force yourself to read if physical or psychological issues distract you. Too much sugar and caffeine and too little sleep can make reading more difficult, and so can certain medications and emotional distractions. If you can't concentrate, return to the materials when you feel better—but be sure to use this advice sparingly. Sometimes, you'll just need to dig in and get it done, regardless of how you feel.

Meeting EXPECTATIONS

The college will expect that I . . .	To meet that expectation, I will . . .
Example: . . . will read the assigned materials before class.	Example: . . . use active- and critical-reading strategies to study the assigned materials before we discuss them in class.
_____	_____
_____	_____
_____	_____
_____	_____

SKIMMING AND SCANNING CAN BE USEFUL TECHNIQUES

Skimming is reading materials quickly and superficially, paying particular attention to the main ideas. Use this method of reading when you first get a reading assignment. Skimming can help you get a feel for the material, including how long it is and how difficult it will be to read.

To skim a text effectively, read the first and last paragraphs, the headings of all main sections, and the first and last sentences of each paragraph. Of course, if time is a factor, you can delete some of the steps or add more (perhaps reading the first and last paragraphs of each section).

Ideally, skimming should be done before in-depth reading, but sometimes, skimming may provide the only chance you have to read the material. If that's the case, be sure to pay attention to the headings of major sections and the first and last paragraphs. Don't be surprised, though, if you miss major ideas that are sandwiched in the middle.

Scanning is looking quickly for a specific item or topic, as you would scan a website for a particular product or a dictionary for a particular word. Scanning also includes examining the table of contents and index of a book to help you find a particular topic.

Like skimming, scanning requires moving your eyes quickly over a page. In contrast to skimming, however, when you scan, you know what you want to find and slow down once you find it. Scanning is particularly useful when reviewing sources to use for a paper. You can determine rather quickly if a source pertains to your topic. Once you scan a text, you can then skim or read it actively.

Part of scanning a text includes examining its parts. For instance, a book consists of several chapters; each chapter consists of several sections; each section consists of several paragraphs; each paragraph consists of a number of sentences; and each sentence consists of a number of words and phrases. As you read, look for connections between the smallest parts of the reading assignment (the words and phrases) and the biggest parts of the assignment (the entire book or chapter). Also be sure to review the other information about a reading assignment, such as the title, author, table of contents, chapter titles, introduction, section headings, headnotes, bibliography, and index.

As discussed later in this chapter, taking notes while you read and using outlines can help you summarize and organize the various parts of a reading assignment, allowing you to better understand its purpose and meaning as a whole and the individual specific points within it.

SQ3R Is a Useful Reading Strategy

In addition to skimming, scanning, and breaking assigned reading materials into parts, also try one of the most popular reading strategies, called SQ3R (Robinson, 1970). SQ3R stands for *survey, question, read, recite,* and *review:*

(S) **Survey:** Before reading a text closely, start by examining the headings, subheadings, graphics, charts, and references, if included.

(Q) **Question:** After looking for these major organizational signposts, either think of or write down the questions you have. One way to generate questions it to turn headings and subheadings into questions. For example, the subheading "SQ3R Reading Strategy" can be turned into the question "What is the SQ3R reading strategy?"

(R1) **Read:** Read each section one at a time, making sure to concentrate on what you have read.

(R2) **Recite:** After reading each section, say aloud what it was about and answer the questions you came up with during the Question stage. You may also want to write your answers on note cards to review later.

(R3) **Review:** After completing the first four steps, you will be ready to review what you have read. Some experts suggest reviewing within 24 hours of reading, while others recommend reviewing what you have read in short sessions over a period of time.

ACTIVE READING ALSO MEANS CRITICAL READING

While you actively read assigned or researched material, you also need to read it critically. In most cases, this will mean rereading the material, especially if it's short. Be sure to allow yourself plenty of time for this activity. At this point in the critical-reading process, you don't necessarily need to answer the questions you raise. Rather, you should look for places within the material where you want to know more, need clarification, or disagree with the author's conclusion.

Questioning who the author is and what purpose he or she has in writing is the place to start. Questions to ask include the following: "Is the author an authority?" "Is he or she credible?" "Does he or she have an agenda or bias that comes through in the writing?"

If the material comes from a magazine, newspaper, or blog, also question the purpose of that source. When considering the source, ask "What is the purpose of presenting this material?" If the material comes from a newspaper, ask "Does it aim to inform or persuade?" and "Does it present only one side of a debate?" If the material comes from a blog or anonymous website, ask "Is it reliable information? or "Is it only someone sharing his or her observations with no intention of providing accurate information?" Writing these questions in the margins of the text or recording them in a notebook will provide a good start to reading critically.

Another important element of *information literacy* is evaluating what you have read for its usefulness. Just because a book, article, or other material mentions a particular topic doesn't mean that it's a relevant source for your study or research. You need to review the content to determine if it will help you answer the specific questions you have. For example, if you have to write an essay explaining why the U.S. Congress includes both the Senate and the House of Representatives, then a website that lists all the members of Congress won't be helpful. Furthermore, if your assignment requires you to argue in favor of a certain law or legislative act, then you need to evaluate the material you read to determine if it provides supporting information.

In this era of Google searches and Wikipedia entries, finding a lot of information about virtually any topic is pretty easy. The challenge is to evaluate the information for both its credibility and its relevance. These skills are crucial for developing information literacy, and they will serve you well in college and throughout the rest of your life.

Check your understanding of the differences between active and critical reading by completing Activity 1, Active versus Critical Reading.

ACTIVITY 1   Active versus Critical Reading

Place an X in the correct column to indicate if each task is part of active or critical reading.

Task	Active?	Critical?
Asking if the author is biased		
Looking up words you are unfamiliar with		
Determining the author's main point		
Considering what information the author did not provide		

TAKING GOOD NOTES WILL HELP YOU BECOME A BETTER READER

As you have learned so far, the act of reading is more than just moving your eyes along a page. In college, especially, reading requires you to use strategies that will help you to retain the information and to think critically about what you have read.

Taking notes as you read—in your textbook or in a notebook—is an excellent way to remember what you have read and to begin the process of critical reading. Writing down key ideas, terms to look up later, and questions that come up as you read will help you stay focused and improve your comprehension.

Writing in the margins of your textbook can be an effective way to take notes, especially if a reading assignment is lengthy. If you don't mind writing directly in your textbook (and don't plan on selling it back to the bookstore), then summarize the main points you have read. Write brief, two- or three-word summaries or questions in the margins to help you make sense of and remember what you have read. Having these brief, marginal summaries will also help you review the material before class and after class when you start studying for an exam.

If you don't want to write in your book but still want to reap the benefits of summarizing the material, write your summaries on a separate sheet of paper or even on sticky notes that can be removed. With either strategy, make sure that you label each piece of paper or note with the chapter title and page number of the book. Another strategy is to use a reading log, which is a list of what you read, when you read it, and how long it took you to complete the reading. You can also use your reading log in conjunction with in-text notes.

Highlighting in your textbook is another method for taking notes on reading material. You can use a highlighter pen to mark important concepts for review, but be careful that you don't highlight too much information. Highlighting the text too much can have the opposite effect of what's intended: Instead of making it easier to understand key terms and information, too much highlighting will make everything seem of equal importance. If you do use a highlighter pen, use it sparingly. For example, don't highlight more than two sentences in a row. A better method is to use highlighting and written summaries together.

THE UNWRITTEN RULES
Of Reading and Note Taking

- **You can't multitask while reading for your classes.** If you have on music or the television while you're reading or if you're constantly checking your phone or computer for emails, texts, or calls, then it will take you at least 30% longer to read the material—and you'll remember less of it. Find a quiet place for reading, and you'll have far better results.

- **Experiment with using technology for note taking before committing to it entirely.** Students are increasingly using laptops and tablet computers to take notes during class or reading. Ask your professor first before using a laptop or tablet computer in class, and always have a backup pad of paper and pencil or pen for note taking if the technology fails.

- **Your notes from one class will serve you well in future classes.** Be sure to keep your notes throughout your academic career, because you never know when you'll need them. For example, your calculus notes may be very helpful when you encounter a challenge in your statistics or economics class during your junior or senior year.

- **Use caution when sharing notes with others.** Talk to your professor about his or her standards of academic integrity as related to students sharing notes. Some professors consider it cheating. Also keep in mind that your classmate may have overlooked important information or misunderstood concepts when taking notes. If you miss a class, getting notes from someone else is rarely a suitable substitute.

Annotating your textbook and writing down critical questions are both methods of further reinforcing what you have read and will help you prepare for listening and note taking in class. To write critical questions about the reading, ask questions such as "How do I know this is true?" and "What else should I consider?" Annotating your textbook with your own notes will not only help you reinforce the main ideas, but it will also help you synthesize the information in ways that will produce connections between concepts, making the material more memorable and more relevant.

Ebooks Are Coming!

Electronic books, or ebooks, have been gaining popularity with students, professors, and libraries, and using them certainly can be more convenient that using printed sources. For example, you may be able to download an ebook on your computer or other handheld device and read it without having to go to the library to check it out. Also, some ebooks can cost less than their traditional, printed counterparts.

Your reading strategy for ebooks may be different than your reading strategy for print books.

Nonetheless, there are some drawbacks to using ebooks, rather than printed books. Using ebooks is dependent on having access to technology, and you can't sell back ebooks, like you can printed texts. You may want to test an ebook reader—using a friend's reader or one at the library—before purchasing your own to use for class.

Strategies for reading an ebook are similar to those for reading a printed text in that you can preview the overall text by examining the table of contents and chapter headings, looking for main ideas, and questioning the authority and accuracy of the text. However, ebooks have additional tools that can make it easier to read actively and critically. For instance, some ebooks allow you to search for certain terms and highlight them in the text. This can be useful if you are trying to find a specific section in the text. Other ebook tools include highlighters and notes that you can use to mark important information and to record your own ideas. Often, these notes and marks can be saved while you have access to the ebook. A print function is included in some ebooks, and although printing the entire book may not be possible, you should be able to print pages that you need.

COMBINING YOUR CLASS AND TEXT NOTES WILL GIVE YOU THE WHOLE PICTURE

One of the challenges you'll encounter as you accumulate notes is that you'll have notes from your textbook and other written course materials plus notes that you've taken during class discussions and lectures. Here are some suggestions for how to integrate all of your notes into a single collection of useful information:

- *Develop an outline for your content.* Integrate your notes from your class and your reading by organizing them using a similar outline based on the key topics or learning objectives they cover. Start with the main headings from your textbook as a possible outline structure, and compare those headings to the organization and structure of your class notes. You may need to add, remove, or modify headings to accommodate your notes from both sources. Once you have an outline, take your class notes and reading notes and place them in the same locations based on their content.

- *Rewrite, photocopy, cut, and paste, as desired.* Once you have an outline structure for your content, you'll have several options for placing all the content in the right location.
- *Rewrite your notes into the new outline structure you created.* Doing this is helpful because in the process of rewriting your notes, you are consciously reviewing them and gaining greater retention of the content in your long-term memory. The downside is that rewriting your notes can take a lot of time.
- *If you typed your notes on a computer, use the "copy" and "paste" functions in your word-processing software program to move content from one location to another.* The benefit of this option is that it's fast and relatively easy. The downsides are that it requires you to type your notes in the first place and you won't review the information as much as you would if you rewrote the notes by hand.
- *If you wrote your notes by hand, make a copy of them using a photocopier.* Then use scissors and tape to cut out and reorganize various sections of content using the outline that you created. The benefit of this approach is that it's faster than rewriting all of your notes. The downside is that the process of cutting and taping the content from one piece of paper to another can be time consuming.

Whichever method you use, remember that the goal of integrating your reading and class notes is to maximize how much you learn about a concept by drawing information from multiple sources. Also, by comparing the content that your professor discussed in class with what you have read, you'll be able to identify those topics that the professor considers most important.

Another benefit of integrating your notes from readings and class is that you'll have a more useful collection of notes to use in subsequent courses. Many of the courses you take during your freshman year are considered *prerequisites,* which means that you'll use the information and skills gained from them to help you in future courses. Keeping good notes will help you refresh your memory in later terms when the concepts reemerge. For example, if you take a precalculus class your first semester, you may need your notes from that class during later semesters when you take calculus.

The process of note taking while reading is an important skill, both for your college success and your career success. Regardless of the kind of career that you intend to pursue, the ability to take effective notes while reading will serve you well, since so much information is communicated using the written word.

Make time to combine your class notes with your reading notes.

INTEGRITY *Matters*

Reading in college is not optional; rather, it is crucial to success. After you make the commitment to enroll in college, follow through by tackling the reading that's part of the experience. You will also need to demonstrate integrity when you do not read. Be honest with your instructor, if asked, and be honest with yourself that your progress (or lack of progress) is related to how well you prepare before class through active and critical reading.

YOUR TURN

In approximately 250 words, describe a time you felt confused in a class because you didn't prepare by reading the assignment beforehand. What happened? • How did you feel? • What did you learn from the experience?

CASE SCENARIOS

1. In high school, Will didn't have to read the textbooks for his classes to pass them. If he just attended class, listened, and took notes, then he could usually do well on the exams. Now Will is in college, but he still believes that it isn't necessary or efficient to read "boring" books when he can find information on the Internet that's presented in a more interesting way. Will is taking math, history, literature, and accounting this semester, and he's proud of the fact that he hasn't bought any textbooks. While he hasn't had a test yet, he thinks he understands everything and even contributes new ideas to class discussions. He doesn't plan to purchase books this semester, because he has friends in each class who have offered to share with him.

    Use the following scale to rate the decision that has been made (1 = Poor Decision, 5 = Excellent Decision). Be prepared to explain your answer.

2. Meghan thinks she may have a reading disability, but she has never been diagnosed. Regardless, she has had to work extra hard to keep up with and understand her reading assignments. She is a single parent and works full time, which means she has little time for tutoring. Meghan also feels that because she has accomplished so much on her own—taking care of her child, holding down a well-paying job, and supporting her youngest sibling through his college career—she can handle her problem on her own. She has checked out a website on reading disabilities and decided to purchase a set of CDs for $150 that promise to help her become a faster reader. Meghan thinks this reading program will help her.

    Use the following scale to rate the decision that has been made (1 = Poor Decision, 5 = Excellent Decision). Be prepared to explain your answer.

    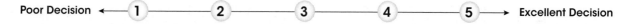

3. Wilson can't remember anything he reads for class, even though he spends hours the night before reading the material. He's also having difficulty remembering what words mean. Although he's slowly building his vocabulary, he still finds himself looking up the same word several times before he can remember its meaning. Wilson has decided to make flashcards for all the new vocabulary he encounters, including words and definitions, and to tape them up all over his apartment. He's even keeping a stack of vocabulary cards in his car in case he finds himself waiting somewhere. He has also bought crossword puzzle books in the hope of increasing his vocabulary.

    Use the following scale to rate the decision that has been made (1 = Poor Decision, 5 = Excellent Decision). Be prepared to explain your answer.

Take It with You

Action Item	Deadline	First Step
Develop a reading preparation plan, including a specific time and location to read.		
Practice the SQ3R reading strategy on a reading assignment.		
Purchase notebooks, pens, and/or pencils for taking notes in each class.		

REFERENCE

Robinson, F.P. (1970). *Effective study* (4th ed.). New York, NY: Harper & Row.

8 Studying and Test Taking

Studying the origins of life in Biology 101 was becoming an exercis in personal survival. Juanita, Evan, Michael, and Laura had forme a study group early in the semester, and it had become a preciou lifeline.

"So much work for just one class!" Michael exclaimed. "It's insane!"

Juanita added, "I'm taking world literature and psychology. The readin alone takes me hours each night."

Michael thought he studied too much about the wrong things, and Juanita had severe test anxiety any time she took a test.

"Are you starting without me?" Laura asked as she dropped her heavy backpack on the booth seat by Michael.

"Of course not," Juanita said. "Michael was just complaining about how much work this class is."

"My mother finished her degree right before I started school, and I remember how much she studied. If she can do it, I thin I can, too," Laura said.

"Does anyone know what the next test will cover?" Michael asked.

"I have to study everything, even if I don't think it will be on the test," said Juanita. "If I'm not overly prepared, I won't do wel I suggest we start going over everything that we've done since the first chapter."

Evan offered his advice: "If we only review our notes, we should be fine. When was the last time you failed a test? You have to get something for just taking it."

This didn't make sense to Laura, so she made a suggestion: "We all seem to have different approaches, so it sounds like we would be better off studying by ourselves."

Juanita, Evan, Michael, and Laura need to develop a plan for studying and taking tests, and so do you. To put you on the path to success, this chapter will help you do the following:

- Develop effective study habits.
- Practice various memory strategies for studying.
- Apply strategies for taking different types of tests.

LEARNING OUTCOME

Recommend strategies for studying for and taking a test.

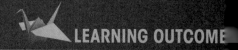

MyStudentSuccessLab (www.mystudentsuccesslab.com) is an online solution designed to help you 'Start strong, Finish stronger' by building skills for ongoing personal and professional development.

STUDYING IS A NECESSARY LIFELONG HABIT

Study groups can be an effective way of preparing for tests if you use them wisely.

As mentioned in an earlier chapter, the book *What Matters in College* (Astin, 1993) provides strong evidence that the amount of time students spend practicing what they're trying to learn (called *time on task*) is *the* single greatest predictor of academic success.

With this in mind, the best advice for taking tests is plain and simple: Study for every test—no exceptions. By studying for every test in every class, you'll develop the habits needed for success in your studies, your career, and your life.

Here are some specific tips for developing effective study habits:

- *Set a time and a place for studying that work well for you.* Put regular, ongoing appointments on your calendar specifically for studying the content from each class you're taking. Begin these appointments the first week of the term.
- *Designate a specific location for studying.* Find a place that's quiet and comfortable and that has good lighting and enough space for your supplies and books. The best location may be away from your dorm, home, or apartment.
- *Make arrangements for your children (if applicable).* Make the most of children's nap and sleep times, or find a reliable babysitter. If you have classmates with similar child-care needs, consider babysitting swaps to give each of you time to study regularly.
- *Set goals for your studying.* Are you trying to memorize content, to understand how a process works, or to solve a math problem? Start each study session by identifying what you're trying to accomplish.
- *Study actively.* Instead of simply rereading notes or passively reviewing the major headings in your textbook, do activities such as the following:
  - Rewriting or summarizing your notes
  - Rearranging the order of materials—for instance, from most important to least important, from least important to most important, in chronological order, and so on

Meeting EXPECTATIONS

The college will expect that I . . .	To meet that expectation, I will . . .
Example: . . . *spend a considerable amount of time studying for tests.*	Example: . . . *work with a study group to prepare for tests.*

- Making connections between what you have learned in one chapter, unit, or class and what you have learned at other times and places
- Making connections between what you have learned in class and what you have experienced in the real world
- Explaining concepts to someone who is not familiar with the topic
- Making visual representations of materials

USING MEMORY STRATEGIES CAN HELP YOU REMEMBER AND LEARN MORE DEEPLY

Research on the human brain has shown that spending more time actively learning a subject can translate into deeper learning and that having a positive attitude toward a challenging learning situation will result in learning more. Why? As you spend more time studying and engaged in active learning with a positive attitude, you'll remember more of what you have learned, because you'll have moved information from your short-term memory to your long-term memory. Those are the two types of memory: short term and long term.

When you meet someone, you keep that person's name and face in your short-term memory. In general, you can store only five to nine items at a time in short-term memory. If you try to add more items, you'll find that some of them slip away (Miller, 1956). Test your short-term memory by completing Activity 1.

ACTIVITY 1 Short-Term Memory Test

Glance at the following chart of words for 30 seconds. Then cover up the list and write down the words you remember. You don't have to list the words in the same order that you've seen them.

cup	paper	pencil	magnet	ruler	scissors
spoon	towel	tape	apple	knife	straw

How well did you do? If you remembered five to nine items, then you can consider your short-term memory average. It takes some work, though, to transfer information from your short-term memory to your long-term memory.

Memorizing Is an Important Skill

Modern technologies—including computers, smart phones, and ebook readers—make it easy for us to have a lot of information at our fingertips. With information so accessible, we might think that we don't need to memorize anything anymore.

The truth is, however, that having effective memorization skills is very important to college success. Quizzes, exams, and other types of tests are often *closed book,* which means that you can't refer to your textbook, notes, or other materials during the test. And because most tests are timed, you don't have enough time anyway to search for information while trying to answer a question. You either know the answer or you don't. For these reasons, it's very important to develop effective memorization skills.

Mnemonic Devices Can Help You Remember

Mnemonic devices are memory aids or strategies that help you remember items, concepts, or series of events. Usually, mnemonic devices are *not* helpful for deep learning, but they are helpful for learning the detailed content that often lays a foundation for deep learning.

Memory can be strengthened by participating in mental activities.

For example, during your college experience, you may need to name all the bones in the human body or all the amendments in the U.S. Constitution. At these times, you may find yourself using mnemonic devices as part of your learning process.

Device 1: The Roman Room

Return to the list of words in Activity 1, and think about how you can remember all the items. The ancient Romans are credited with being able to remember significant amounts of information by using a technique called the *Roman Room*, also known as the *Memory Palace* and *loci method* (Foer, 2007). This visualization technique can be useful when trying to remember a string of seemingly unrelated items or complex materials that need to be pulled together.

To create a Roman Room, visualize a familiar place, such as a room in your house. If the room is connected to other rooms, then you will have more "places" to put ideas. When you visualize your room, pay particular attention to the items that are already in the room, such as furniture or favorite pictures, and to the room's unique details, such as peeling paint. The more vivid the visualization, the better able you will be to remember the items you place in the room.

To see the Roman Room or loci method in action, complete Activity 2.

ACTIVITY 2   **Roman Room**

Take another look at the same chart of words:

cup	paper	pencil	magnet	ruler	scissors
spoon	towel	tape	apple	knife	straw

Now think about placing these items in your kitchen. Put the *straw* in the *cup* and place them both in the cabinet. *Tape* the *paper* on the front of the cabinet. Place the *towel* on the counter next to the *apple*, *spoon*, and *knife*. Then put the *pencil*, *ruler*, *magnet*, and *scissors* in the drawer.

Take 30 seconds to describe the kitchen, or describe your own Roman Room with the items listed. Then cover up both the list and the description of the room, and see how many items you can remember. Write the words on a separate piece of paper.

Did you remember more words this time? If not, then visualization may not be the only type of mnemonic device you need to help remember a lot of detailed information.

Device 2: Acronyms and Acrostic Sentences

Other mnemonic devices may benefit students with different learning style preferences. Acronyms and acrostic sentences are two methods that may help students with a verbal learning style preference.

To form an acrostic sentence, take the first letter of each item in a series to create a descriptive sentence that helps you remember the items and their order. For example, music students remember the order of the notes on the lines of the treble clef staff (E, G, B, D, F) with the sentence "Every Good Boy Does Fine." To recall the order of biological groupings used in taxonomy (Kingdom, Phylum, Class, Order, Family, Genus, Species), students remember "Kids Prefer Cheese Over Fried Green Spinach."

To create an acronym, take the first letter of each item in a series and form another word or string of characters. Acronyms that we use every day include AIDS (acquired immune deficiency syndrome), SADD (Students Against Drunk Driving), REM (rapid eye movement), and SCUBA (self-contained underwater breathing apparatus). Acronyms that many students have used to help remember terms and the orders of items include ROY G BIV (the colors in the rainbow: red, orange, yellow, green, blue, indigo, and violet) and FACE (the notes in the spaces of the treble clef staff).

The list you've worked with contains too many words to create an acronym, but you can create an acrostic sentence (or two) using the initial letter of each word. Do this by completing Activity 3.

ACTIVITY 3 **Acrostic Sentences**

Write one or two acrostic sentences using these letters:

C	P	P	M	R	S
S	T	T	A	K	S

The order of the items isn't important, so feel free to rearrange the letters to make your sentence(s).

Here's an example sentence using the letters in the first row:

Creative People Produce Many Real Skits.

Device 3: Rhymes and Songs

Rhymes and songs are another type of mnemonic device. Although they are a little more difficult to compose than acronyms and acrostics, they often appeal to auditory learners. Who doesn't remember sayings such as "Thirty days hath September . . ." (to name the days in the months) and "In 1492, Columbus sailed the ocean blue" (to recall the year that Columbus set out for the New World)?

Again, these memory strategies work best for learning simple information. It will take more work to remember the cultural and economic effects of Columbus's discovery of the New World, for example.

Device 4: Chunking

Ideally, you will take time to explore a variety of memory strategies, trying them out until you find the one that works best for the subject matter and your own learning style preference. But if you're like many students, you'll need a memory strategy to work quickly as you cram before a test.

Students who cram may be successful in remembering content when they take the test the following day, but they won't likely remember the content weeks, months, or years later. That's why professors and tutors discourage students from cramming. It may work some of the time, and it's better than not studying at all for a test. Regardless, cramming often produces additional anxiety and stress, and the material you learn will not likely be stored in your long-term memory when you need it later.

With this warning in mind, consider that at some time, despite your best intentions, you will need to learn key concepts in a short amount of time. To do so, you should learn a fail-safe memory technique.

One method, called *chunking*, is similar to the Roman Room or loci method in that items are grouped to allow the brain to make connections with them, making it easier to recall the information later. The goal in chunking is to reduce a large number of items to only five to nine items. To see chunking in action, try to memorize the following 10-digit number:

You may find it easier to remember the number by chunking the digits the way a phone number is divided:

511–479–6210

You probably don't realize that you chunk any time you memorize a phone number or account number (such as your bank account or Social Security number). In each case, you take a series of seemingly random numbers and put them together in groups.

To practice this mnemonic technique, do Activity 4, in which you memorize a variety of memory-related terms.

ACTIVITY 4 **Chunking**

Use the following list of key terms:

acrostic	mnemonic device
acronym	rhyme
chunking	Roman Room
cramming	short-term memory
loci method	teaching others
long-term memory	

First, make sure that you know the definition of each term. Record the definition next to each term:

acrostic _____

acronym _____

chunking _____

cramming _____

loci method _____

long-term memory _____

mnemonic device _____

rhyme _____

Roman Room _____

short-term memory _____

teaching others _____

Next, group the items logically. Then, complete the chunking with the remaining terms. For example, here's one way to group some of the terms:

Mnemonic devices are strategies for remembering items, and they include **acrostics, acronyms, rhymes,** and **Roman Rooms.**

How else could the terms be chunked? Use a separate sheet of paper to group them in various ways.

DIFFERENT TESTS AND TEST QUESTIONS REQUIRE USING DIFFERENT STRATEGIES

Although the terms *test* and *exam* are often used interchangeably, they have slightly different meanings. A *test* is a set of questions or problems that are used to evaluate one's skills, aptitudes, and abilities on a certain topic. Usually, a test assesses students'

THE UNWRITTEN RULES

Of Studying and Taking Tests

- **Cramming for a test or pulling an all-nighter is rarely useful.** If you try to study for a test just a day or a few hours in advance, you won't remember much of what you study. Also, the stress caused by your procrastination will probably deplete your ability to think creatively and critically.

- **Credit is credit, even if it's partial credit.** Suppose you have to answer an essay question that's worth 20 points, and you're confident that you know part of the answer but not all of it. Take the time to do well on the part that you know so you will get some credit for the answer.

- **Prepare yourself for the test conditions as much as the test itself.** Depending on your university's schedule, each of your final exams may take as long as three hours. When's the last time that you actually sat in one place for three hours working on a test or exam? You wouldn't think of preparing for a marathon by running 100-yard sprints, so don't prepare for a three-hour exam by practicing in 20- or 30-minute sessions. The only way to perform well during a lengthy exam is to prepare yourself for thinking and writing for that block of time.

- **After the professor hands out the exam, if you don't understand a question, ask privately for clarification.** It will be up to the professor to decide how much help and clarification to provide, but it never hurts to ask. Don't start writing your answer until you completely understand the question.

- **Really long answers are rarely really good answers.** When faced with an essay question about a broad topic, students are tempted to write everything they know about it in the hope that something they write will satisfy the professor. This is the "everything but the kitchen sink" essay answer. This type of answer is rarely effective. To write a good essay response, pay attention to the verb or verbs used in the question. Being asked to *compare* is different from being asked to *evaluate*. Then write an answer that directly answers the question in a complete but concise manner.

knowledge and skills related to part of a course. An *exam,* however, is by definition an assessment of the content of an entire course or program. *Final exams* are sometimes called *comprehensive* or *cumulative exams,* because they cover what students have studied all semester or term.

Unless your professor tells you directly what will be on a test, assume that anything he or she assigned or covered in class may be included. Just about every college student has a story about taking a test that covered only the reading assignments and not what was discussed in class. These students were surprised to realize that studying their lecture notes wasn't enough to do well on the test.

The following is a list of materials that you may be "fair game" for a test in any class:

- Materials from lectures, discussion, and in- and out-of-class activities
- Information provided by guest speakers
- Information from workshops or field trips
- Information from multimedia productions, such as videos and audios
- Content from assigned readings, including chapters in the textbook and other publications
- Materials from handouts, including PowerPoint slides and outlines

You can also be assured of encountering a variety of types of tests and test questions. Take clues from what you do in class to help determine what kinds of tests and questions you may come across. For example, if your professor spends time applying information from a chapter during class or has you do this as an assignment, then he or she will likely prepare test questions that ask you to apply the information, as well. Listen for clues that professors give, such as "You should write this down" and "This is a really important point." Other cue phrases include "You may see this again on a test" and "If you saw this problem on a test, how would you answer it?" When you

It's in the SYLLABUS

Look at each class syllabus for clues about the tests you will have. Consider these questions:

- What types of test questions do you anticipate?

- What evidence in the syllabus leads you to believe you will have certain types of test questions? (*Hint:* Look at the course description, if included.)

- How often will you have tests?

hear these phrases, write them down and review them when studying your other notes. A professor who says these things is begging you to take note!

Test Questions Will Vary, and So Should Your Answers

There are two general categories of question types: objective and subjective. *Objective* questions usually require lower-level thinking. They ask you to recall facts and concepts, usually in the forms of multiple-choice, true/false, fill-in-the-blank, and short-answer questions. *Subjective* questions ask for your opinions about the content or ask you to apply the content in new ways. Essay and problem-solving (critical-thinking) questions are considered subjective, because they can be answered correctly in a variety of ways.

Sometimes, objective questions are easier to answer because the correct answer is included among the set of choices that's provided. However, answering objective questions can demand significant brainpower, especially when you must provide an answer for a question that gives very few clues, which is often the case with fill-in-the-blank questions. Since objective questions usually have single correct answers, some students believe that subjective questions have no wrong answers. While that may be somewhat true, there are effective ways to answer subjective questions. The following sections discuss typical types of test questions and how to answer them.

Multiple Choice

When answering a multiple-choice question, the first step is to read the question or statement carefully. Mark any special words in the question or statement that are keys to its meaning, such as *not, always,* and *only.*

Next, read each answer choice carefully, and eliminate any that are obviously wrong. If you have to guess, eliminate any answer with a misspelled or incorrect term (usually a sign that the instructor has hurriedly added false answers) and any answer that's shorter than the others. Also pay attention to choices such as "All of the above" and "None of the above." If you can determine that at least two of the choices are correct, then "All of the above" is probably the correct answer. Likewise, if at least two of the choices are incorrect, then "None of the above" is probably the correct answer.

When studying for a test that will include multiple-choice questions, be sure you know all the materials well. Also practice answering multiple-choice questions by using those in your textbook (or on a companion textbook website, if one is available) or creating your own multiple-choice questions based on the materials you are studying. Work through the questions alone, or share and practice with a classmate who has also created multiple-choice questions.

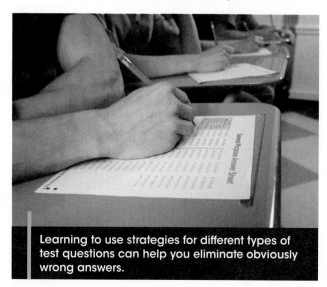

Learning to use strategies for different types of test questions can help you eliminate obviously wrong answers.

Matching

The matching section on a test usually presents two columns of information: a list of words or phrases and a list of descriptors. Your goal is to match corresponding items from the two columns—a term with its definition, for instance.

Professors who use matching sections usually require the basic recall of information, but you should read the directions carefully. There may be more than one match for an item in the list, or there may be extra descriptors that do not match anything. These *distractors* are included to make sure you know the content well enough to make the right decisions.

To complete a matching section, first read through both lists of information. Try to determine if there might be multiple matches or extra descriptors. In recording your answers, make sure that you write down the correct letter to match each word or phrase in the list. If you don't know some of the answers, use the process of elimination to narrow down the possible choices by first matching the terms you know for sure. Also, when the terms are of different types (for instance, some are people, some are places, some are dates), you may be able to eliminate certain descriptors because they don't logically match up.

To study for matching questions, you will need to know major terms, people, and events from the class materials. Also keep in mind that professors often use definitions and descriptions that are similar to the ones in the text or glossary, rather than the ones directly from this kind of source, to test your understanding of the content. It may be helpful to rewrite your definitions and descriptions in your own words. If you have a study partner or group, ask them to do the same and share the answers they record.

True/False

True/false questions can be tough, even though they have only two possible answers: true or false. Guessing or randomly answering true/false questions should be done as a last resort. A better approach is to read each statement carefully, noting key words and phrases that could point to the correct answer, such as *frequently, sometimes,* and *a few.* These words and phrases usually indicate a true statement. Words such as *never, only,* and *always* usually indicate a false statement.

If you're struggling with a particular true/false statement, take a moment to "flip" the statement and see if your answer would switch from true to false or false to true. Using this strategy can help you work through double negatives and other confusing language.

To study for true/false test questions, use the study tips provided earlier for multiple-choice and matching questions. Your goal is to know the course material or content well enough that when you're presented with questions about it, you can recognize major concepts and questions. Also try writing out sample true/false questions that you think would make good additions to the test. Share them with a study partner or group, and take turns answering each other's sample questions.

Fill-in-the-Blank/Short Answer

Fill-in-the-blank and short-answer questions require you to recall specific information, such as definitions of key terms or items in a series. To complete these types of questions, first read the sentence or question carefully. Often, you will lose points for the question if you don't answer it exactly or misspell the correct term.

Fill-in-the-blank and short-answer questions can be particularly difficult if you aren't familiar enough with the materials. A good way to study for these questions is to create and use flash cards, which have a term or major concept on one side and a definition or description of the term or concept on the other side.

Problem Solving

Instructors use problem-solving, or critical-thinking, questions to have students demonstrate or apply the concepts or ideas they have learned. To answer a problem-solving question, first read the question carefully. Mark multiple steps or parts to the directions. Next, determine what information you'll need to solve the problem. Then, break

INTEGRITY *Matters*

Nearly 75% of college students admit to cheating at least once, as reported by Plagiarism.org (2012) and other sources. The reasons students give for cheating are many: Some don't believe that their professors notice or care about their work, while others believe that getting good grades is the most important goal, given the high standards demanded by scholarships and program admissions (such as nursing schools). Colleges do take cheating seriously, however, and often have no tolerance for students who cheat. Penalties can range from getting an F in the course to being expelled.

YOUR TURN

In approximately 250 words, describe why you think such a high percentage of college students have reported cheating. Also describe what colleges can do to help maintain an environment of academic integrity.

the problem into parts, and write down what process or operation you will need to perform. Work through the problem, and after you arrive at an answer, check the directions again to make sure you have adequately answered it.

Studying for a problem-solving test, such as a math or science test, will most likely involve practicing similar types of problems. Work through the additional problems in your textbook, homework assignments, and notes for extra practice. You may also find sample problems online, with answers provided so that you can check yourself.

Essay Questions

Instructors use essay questions to measure students' ability to analyze, synthesize, and evaluate the concepts they have learned. Essay questions evaluate much more than students' recall of facts or terms. You can be assured that you'll encounter many essay questions in college, because they allow students to demonstrate a deeper understanding of the materials.

In an exam context, the term *essay* can also refer to a question requiring a detailed, well-developed answer that uses material from the course to support a particular thesis or to describe a particular concept. Your answers to essay questions should not be based on your own opinions (unless the professor specifically asks for your opinions). Instead, your answers should demonstrate your understanding and recall of important information from the class (such as textbook readings and lecture notes) to address particular challenges or to explain certain ideas. Another important thing to remember about essay questions is that although you won't have a lot of time to answer them, your professor will still expect your responses to be thorough and clear.

To answer an essay question, always begin by reading the directions carefully. If the question has more than one part, be sure to mark each part and then answer it in the body of the essay. If the directions specify a length requirement (a number of words), be sure to meet or exceed it. And before you begin writing, create a brief outline of what you will cover in the essay.

Study for essay questions just as you would problem-solving questions by practicing. If your professor provides a list of topics or sample questions, use them to create outlines and then memorize the outlines. They will serve as the bases for your essays. If you don't receive sample topics or questions, then create your own by reviewing the course materials and your notes to identify topics that were emphasized in class or that you spent the most time on. These may be clues to possible essay questions.

CASE SCENARIOS

1. Sylvia's accounting professor announced to the class that he allows students to study from old tests. In fact, he provides a folder of previously used tests in the library for students to review. One of Sylvia's classmates, Maria, asked her if she wanted to study for the test, and she agreed. When the two met, Maria pulled out a copy of a test with the current semester's date on it. Sylvia questioned her, and Maria said that the professor gave her a rough draft of a test he decided not to use. When Sylvia went to class and took the test, she recognized every question, because the test was the same one that Maria had shown her. Sylvia decided to take the test without saying anything to her professor.

   Use the following scale to rate the decision that has been made (1 = Poor Decision, 5 = Excellent Decision). Be prepared to explain your answer.

   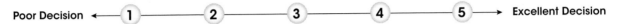
   Poor Decision ← 1 —— 2 —— 3 —— 4 —— 5 → Excellent Decision

2. Ryan glided through high school without cracking open a book, but now that he's in college, he's realized that he doesn't know how to study very well. He's taking five classes: Intermediate Algebra, Reading Improvement, Introduction to Sociology, Speech Communication, and Concepts of Health and Wellness. Although it's early in the semester, he's already struggling through his health and math classes and has made low C's and a D on recent tests. Eager to do better, Ryan has asked some classmates to get together over beer and pizza to study for the rest of the semester.

   Use the following scale to rate the decision that has been made (1 = Poor Decision, 5 = Excellent Decision). Be prepared to explain your answer.

   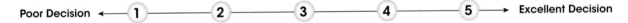
   Poor Decision ← 1 —— 2 —— 3 —— 4 —— 5 → Excellent Decision

3. Betty gets sweaty palms and feels like throwing up each time she has to take a test. She has actually failed and dropped classes because she couldn't calm down enough to take major tests. This semester, though, Betty wants to do better. She can't keep dropping and failing classes! Betty has talked to her classmates about what they do to ease test anxiety. One told her about an herbal tea drink that calms your nerves but makes make you very sleepy a few hours later. Another friend suggested taking an energy supplement to pep her up and keep her from worrying. Betty has decided to drink the tea before taking her test.

   Use the following scale to rate the decision that has been made (1 = Poor Decision, 5 = Excellent Decision). Be prepared to explain your answer.

   Poor Decision ← 1 —— 2 —— 3 —— 4 —— 5 → Excellent Decision

Take It with You

Action Item	Deadline	First Step
Schedule blocks of time on your calendar system for studying.		
Identify a specific location for studying.		
Complete practice tests.		

REFERENCES

Astin, A.W. (1993). *What matters in college.* San Francisco: Jossey-Bass.

Foer, J. (2007). Remember this. *National Geographic* 212(5), 32–55.

Miller, G. (1956). The magical number seven, plus or minus two: Some limits on our capacity for processing information. Retrieved from http://www.musanim.com/miller1956

Plagiarism.org. (2012). Did you know? Retrieved from http://www.plagiarism.org/plag_article_did_you_know.html

9 Communication and Diversity

"Evan, are you going to be around later today?" Michael asked. "I may need some help."

Michael had felt an instant connection with Evan the day they met, probably because Evan was a lot like him—athletic, driven, and still unsure of himself as a college student.

"Sure," Evan said. "Maybe you can help me, too. Think you can lend me a hand with some furniture?"

"Are you sure you can use help from me?" Michael asked.

Michael had never thought much about being older than other students until recently, when some classmates said something about his being "too old" to work with on their assigned group project.

"You may be older," Evan replied, laughing, "but I'm pretty sure you can bench-press more than me."

"Maybe when I was your age, but not anymore," Michael replied. "Seriously, though, I have this group project, and my group keeps meeting without me. I just have to do well on it."

"Ah, c'mon," Evan said. "I would make you the leader of the group. I've heard you debate others and win. You are fierce in an argument."

"I think that's part of the problem," Michael said. "I don't know. Maybe I come on too strong and offend people. I ran into a guy in my class, and he said he saw two members of my group meeting in the library—without me."

"So what do you need from me? Some boxing tips, maybe?" Evan asked.

"No, I think the best thing to do is to find a new group. I'm sure my professor will understand, given the situation," answered Michael.

Like Michael, you'll need to navigate the opportunities and challenges of communicating and working with others during your college career. This chapter will help you to do the following:

- Tailor your communication to accommodate a diverse audience.
- Create and participate in teams.
- Manage conflict in one-on-one and team settings.

LEARNING OUTCOME

Recommend strategies to communicate effectively with diverse audiences, including peers, instructors, and team members.

MyStudentSuccessLab (www.mystudentsuccesslab.com) is an online solution designed to help you 'Start strong, Finish stronger' by building skills for ongoing personal and professional development.

YOUR COMMUNICATION NEEDS TO FIT A DIVERSE AUDIENCE

It's in the SYLLABUS

Review the syllabi for your classes, and determine what information is provided that will help you better communicate with your professors. Consider these questions:

- What are your professors' office hours?
- How do your professors prefer to be contacted when you have questions?
- What are the expectations regarding meeting with your professors?

In college, as in life, your ability to communicate with others is one of the most important skills that you can develop. People who can listen and understand the ideas and feelings of others and who can communicate their own ideas and feelings effectively to others are able to succeed in life and maintain healthy relationships. In contrast, people who have a difficult time communicating their own thoughts and feelings and who aren't good at listening to and understanding others often find themselves struggling in many areas of their lives. To put it simply, being able to communicate—through speaking, writing, and listening—is one of the most important skills that you can develop during your college experience.

Communication is a process, and to understand it, you should break it down into the "Who?" "What?" "How?" and "Why?" (see also Exhibit 1):

- *"Who?"* includes the people who are communicating—the sender and the receiver (or senders and receivers, if the communication is in a group setting).
- *"What?"* is the message—the actual content and meaning of what the sender is trying to convey to the receiver.
- *"How?"* is the method used by the sender to convey the message and its meaning. The method might involve speaking, writing, or using nonverbal communication (such as facial gestures or tone of voice).
- *"Why?"* is the intent or motive of the sender. We can each probably remember a time when we spoke or wrote something with the intent of hurting someone's feelings, but we can also remember a time when we were trying to help someone but he or she responded with hurt feelings. Such situations help us realize that while our intent or motive affects how and what we communicate, we don't have complete control over how the receiver interprets or responds to our message.

In light of the "Who?" "What?" "How?" and "Why?" of communication, one of your challenges and opportunities in college is to learn how to modify and adjust your communication to suit your audience (that is, the receiver or receivers). In college, you'll engage in communication with a variety of people: other students; professors, staff, and administrators; employers and coworkers; and friends, family, and other loved ones. On any given day, you may find yourself communicating with very different people in very different situations. To communicate effectively with all these people and in all these situations, learn how to adjust your communication to help achieve your goals and

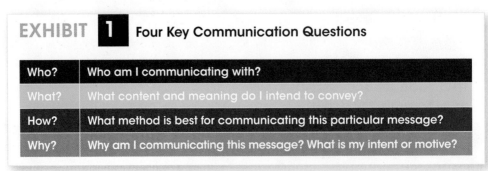

EXHIBIT 1	Four Key Communication Questions
Who?	Who am I communicating with?
What?	What content and meaning do I intend to convey?
How?	What method is best for communicating this particular message?
Why?	Why am I communicating this message? What is my intent or motive?

Developing cultural competence means learning to appreciate diversity.

intentions. To prepare yourself for effectively communicating with diverse audiences, consider what *diversity* is and how it might be represented on your campus.

Value Diversity and Develop Cultural Competence

An exciting part of college is meeting and working with people from all ages and backgrounds. Universities attract individuals from a wide variety of backgrounds and, thus, with a broad spectrum of opinions and beliefs. Your college experience offers you a great opportunity to learn how to live, learn, and work with people who are very different from you in some ways but similar to you in other ways, as well.

A simple definition of the term *diversity* is "difference" or "variety." Another term often heard when diversity is discussed in a college setting is *multiculturalism*. Although the two words have different meanings, they are often used with the same motivation: to expose the university community to a variety of ideas, cultures, viewpoints, beliefs, and backgrounds.

Recognize and Appreciate Diversity in Gender and Sexual Orientation

You will encounter gender diversity at your college. What this means for you is that you will have many opportunities to work with both men and women and to explore any preconceptions you may have about the differences between genders. You may begin to pay more attention to society's assumptions about gender and be more attuned to how language, arts, and sciences, among other disciplines, perpetuate gender stereotypes.

Sexual orientation is another type of diversity that you will more than likely encounter in college, if you haven't already. Homosexuality and bisexuality are two types of sexual orientation diversity. Organizations such as the Human Rights Campaign (www .hrc.org) strive to educate people about the discrimination that can and does occur because of stereotypes and prejudice regarding sexual orientation.

INTEGRITY *Matters*

Integrity is related to trust. You want to be able to trust others, and you want others to be able to trust you. As you build friendships in college, your friends might share things about themselves that are private or sensitive, such as health issues, sexual orientation, and relationship problems. How you handle that information will greatly affect your relationship with that person and whether people consider you trustworthy.

YOUR TURN

In approximately 250 words, describe a time you demonstrated trustworthiness by keeping private some information that an individual shared with you. Discuss the effects of the experience and how you felt about it.

Why should you learn more about sexual orientation as a part of diversity? Sexuality is part of the human experience, and one purpose of higher education is to help you better understand and appreciate your human experience, as well as the experiences of others. Recognizing sexual orientation as a category of diversity gives you a more complete picture of humankind.

Racial, Ethnic, and Cultural Diversity Support Development of Cultural Competence

A person who possesses cultural competence is able to work effectively in cross-cultural situations with people who have experiences, backgrounds, and beliefs that are different than one's own. It's important for you to develop cultural competence because the demographic profile of our planet is changing in dramatic ways that affect you wherever you live. The population growth in countries such as China and India, the increase in the U.S. Hispanic population, and the growth of the world's Muslim population are just a few examples of demographic trends that will affect not only your college experience but also your career and personal life well beyond college. Learning to communicate and work well with individuals who have different demographic profiles than your own is a critical skill for lifelong learning.

The university environment provides the ideal place for you to meet people of diverse cultures and backgrounds. Be proactive and seek out these opportunities whenever possible. You may feel intimidated at first, especially if you recognize that you are lacking in certain aspects of cultural competence. But just as the citizens of a foreign country appreciate it when a visitor attempts to speak in their language (even if it's done somewhat poorly), so will the people of different cultures with whom you engage appreciate your efforts to learn more about them and their perspectives.

Generational Diversity Is More Prevalent Than Ever

You will no doubt encounter generational diversity both at your college and in the world of work—in fact, more so than people from generations past. A *generational cohort* is a group of people that were born within a certain period of time, that identify some of the same world events as important, and that share certain values

(Zemke, Raines, & Filipczak, 2000). The values shared by members of a generational cohort influence how they work with others and how they achieve and perceive personal success.

During your college experience, you will have classmates, professors, employers, coworkers, and friends from different generations than your own. Embrace this wonderful opportunity to learn how to work with people who have different perspectives on life than you do. The key to accepting generational diversity, as with all types of diversity, is to learn more about yourself and others and appreciate the differences.

Don't Overlook Socioeconomic Diversity

The forms of diversity discussed so far—gender and sexual orientation; ethnic, racial, and cultural; and generational—tend to be based on observable characteristics that we recognize in people when we meet them. Other forms of diversity are less visible but no less important, including socioeconomic diversity. The students, faculty, staff, and administrators who gather within your university community come from a wide variety of social and economic backgrounds, and this form of diversity provides yet another enrichment opportunity for your college experience.

Because of differences in socioeconomic background, the student sitting next to you may have a very different set of beliefs, attitudes, abilities, experiences, and motivations than you do. These differences may have little to do with the student's physical characteristics and far more to do with his or her experiences growing up in a relatively poor or wealthy family—or a family from a different socioeconomic class than your own.

To help you explore this dimension of diversity even more, take a look at the book *Bridges Out of Poverty,* by Ruby K. Payne, Philip DeVol, and Terie Dreussi Smith (2000).

Adjusting Your Communication to Accommodate Diversity

Now that you have a more complete perspective on the types of diversity you might encounter on campus, think about how you might need to adjust your communication to accommodate the differences among people. Recall the "Who?" "What?" "How?" and "Why?" of communication discussed earlier. As you encounter diversity, you'll see that "Who" you are communicating with might lead you to adjust "What" you say or write, "How" you say or write it, and "Why" you are communicating in the first place.

For example, take the difference between communicating with your professor and communicating with one of your classmates, and use email as the form of communication. When you are sending email to a classmate, you likely use conversational forms of expression and an informal style of

Your institution may provide you exposure to a variety of different people.

Meeting EXPECTATIONS

The college will expect that I ...	To meet that expectation, I will ...
Example: . . . *value diversity of viewpoints and perspectives.*	Example: . . . *listen to others' ideas with an open mind so that I can understand their points of view, even if they are different from my own.*

communicating, because these qualities reflect how you would talk to the classmate if he or she were sitting next to you in class. But when you are communicating with your professor via email, you would be well advised to communicate in a formal manner, to proofread your writing, to use full sentences and avoid abbreviations and slang, and to convey respect for authority. Because the "Who?" is different, the "What?" "How?" and "Why?" of your communication will be different, too.

Similarly, when you communicate with individuals who are different from you in terms of any form of diversity (such as gender, ethnicity, socioeconomic), adjust your communication to help ensure that they fully understand the meaning you are trying to convey and to prevent them from misinterpreting your intent.

Does all this talk about adjusting your communication to accommodate a diverse audience make you nervous about perhaps saying something wrong? Don't worry! If you make the effort to learn about people who are different from you, to spend time with them, and to talk with them, then you'll develop great relationships. Just being thoughtful and considerate of how others might be different from you will help you immensely in getting along with them.

Recognizing that a classmate may not understand English as well as you or that a coworker is a different age than you will help you recognize the need to adjust your communication accordingly. The most important factor is that by recognizing differences, you are also respecting those differences and making the extra effort to communicate effectively.

SUCCESS IN COLLEGE TAKES A TEAM EFFORT

Teamwork. It's a term you've probably heard a lot, and it probably generates a mixed response on your part. In some ways, working with teams provides a great experience, because you can complete projects, compete in events, and experience various activities in a social setting, sharing the work and responsibilities. In other ways, team experiences can be challenging—for instance, when team members have conflicts with each other, disrupt the group's efforts, or fail to fulfill their responsibilities.

Whatever feelings you might have about teams, your most important realization should be that your future success in your personal life and career will depend, in large part, on your ability to work well in teams. Whether you dream of being a doctor, lawyer, veterinarian, teacher, professional athlete, social worker, or website developer, you will work in teams. And given trends such as the increasing use of communication technology (including videoconferencing and social media), the scattering of technical workers across the globe, and the shifting demographic patterns in the United States, it's likely that you'll work with teams that span different cultures, countries, and careers. In other words, you should plan on working in teams throughout your life—teams that consist of people who have different backgrounds and perspectives from you and who may live in places all over the planet.

Having Successful Group Projects

So, how do you succeed in a team environment in college? First, review the information that you received from your instructor about the group project and its requirements. Having a clear understanding of what your goal is will make it easier to begin your work as a team. Also note the expectations for teamwork. For example, will team members be assigned roles? Will team members evaluate one another at the conclusion of the project? Get clarification from your professor about these matters now, instead of waiting until later in the semester.

Sometimes, it makes sense to assign team members to certain responsibilities based on their experiences or interests. For example, one team member might be an exceptional writer, so he or she might be the best choice for formatting and proofreading each version of the paper. Also designate one or two team members to assume the primary leadership role in overseeing the project and its completion.

Meet early in the term and establish a regular meeting schedule for your team. Compare schedules and find a regular time (such as every Thursday from 11:00 A.M. to 12:00 P.M.) when every team member is expected to attend. Many teams wait too long to have their first meeting and get off to a late start. Even if your project isn't due until the end of the term, meet early in the term to set a course for success on the project or assignment.

Soon after your team has been established, develop a communication system so that everyone on the team always knows what's happening. One system is to have someone on the team take notes during every meeting (a responsibility that could rotate among team members) and to distribute those notes to members via email immediately after every meeting. It's best to communicate with each other clearly and often, preferably in writing.

Also identify both goals and deadlines for your team. What do you have to accomplish and when? Confirming goals and deadlines in writing will help bring the team together toward a shared purpose.

As a team, schedule regular meetings with your professor, as well. Initially, meet with your professor to review the assignment or project requirements and to make sure that everyone on the team has the same understanding. Then later, meet with your professor to review early drafts of your paper or project. Some professors are willing to read initial drafts and provide preliminary feedback, which can really help you improve your final version. You might also need to meet with your professor to help resolve team conflicts that emerge.

Build into your timeline enough lead time to develop several drafts of your written assignment or oral presentation and to finalize the final version of your work. Producing several drafts can give your team the time not only to get instructor feedback but also to review your work yourselves and to refine it before turning in the final copy. Rehearsing an oral presentation well in advance of the formal presentation date will also result in a much better final version (and a better grade) than if you wait until the last minute to prepare and practice.

Finally, before any conflicts among team members occur, develop a process for how to resolve them. In general, when a conflict occurs between two team members, those individuals should attempt to resolve the conflict directly before bringing the issue to

---

EXHIBIT **2** **Tips for Effective Teamwork**

1. Understand the professor's expectations for the project and for team members.
2. Meet with your team early in the term and on a regular, ongoing schedule.
3. Develop a communication system for team members.
4. Schedule regular meetings as a team with your professor.
5. Build lead time into your schedule to complete drafts of a paper or to practice an oral presentation.
6. Develop a process for resolving conflicts—before one occurs.

---

the attention of other team members. If the two team members can't resolve the conflict on their own, then they should bring the conflict to the team as a whole, and the team leaders should attempt to provide some kind of resolution. If the team leaders are unsuccessful in their efforts, then the team should schedule a meeting with the professor to fully discuss the issue and to seek the professor's help in resolving the situation. By following this "lowest level of conflict" approach and starting with the two people in conflict, most problems can be resolved quickly and easily, without involving the entire team.

By following these recommendations for effective teamwork, you'll discover that you can accomplish more work and higher-quality work with a team—whether at school, at home, or at work—than you can individually. Also see Exhibit 2 for tips on effective teamwork. Teams are powerful, and with the right management approach, they can be quite effective, too.

CONFLICT WILL HAPPEN, SO BE READY TO RESOLVE IT

While in college, you may find yourself involved in a conflict that must be resolved for you to be successful and satisfied. The conflict may arise between you and a family member, a classmate, a roommate, or even a professor. How you handle the conflict may have long-term consequences for your academic and lifelong success.

Many times, a minor conflict, such as a miscommunication or misunderstanding, can be resolved easily. Other times, resolving a disagreement may require more time and effort and perhaps the help of others.

Boundaries Provide Healthy Limits

Because you will be surrounded by a diverse group of people, it may be difficult for you to create and maintain the traditional boundaries that exist between students and their counselors, professors, administrators, and learning support staff. Even so, setting boundaries is necessary.

What are *boundaries*? As explained by Cloud and Townsend (1992), a *boundary* is a property line that defines the beginning and end of what we own and what others own. In the context of relationships, boundaries help us understand who owns or is responsible for feelings, attitudes, and behaviors.

The idea of setting boundaries when you are getting to know others may seem backward or contradictory. Why should you avoid forming close relationships with professors and advisors? Don't you *want* them to get to know you in case you need to ask for a referral or recommendation someday? Help your professors and advisors get to know you through your work as a student. Set and maintain clear boundaries in developing these relationships.

Solving Problems Requires Following Procedures

No matter how well you define your boundaries and work hard to maintain good relationships with the people around you, conflicts will occur. In preparation for conflict, it's helpful to establish processes and procedures for your personal use and to know the procedures that your professor and university have established for the classroom and the campus. Universities tend to have well-established processes and procedures to help students, professors, and staff members resolve almost any kind of conflict. Knowing and following these procedures will ensure that a problem is handled appropriately and quickly.

Learning to work well with others, regardless of how different they are from you, and complete tasks as a team is an important skill to develop in college.

The first step to resolving a conflict in class is to define the problem. Is it a communication problem? Is it a problem with the grading standards in the course? Do you feel like a team member isn't fulfilling his or her responsibilities? Whatever the case, when you define the problem, be sure to acknowledge anything that you did to contribute to it. Conflicts can often be disarmed simply by having both people acknowledge their mistakes and express their desire to resolve the problem.

THE UNWRITTEN RULES
Of Communication and Diversity

- **Students who learn to communicate with diverse audiences are better equipped to succeed in their lives and careers.** If you attend college at a campus that's extremely diverse by any definition, the practice and experience you'll gain from learning to communicate in this environment will set you up well for future success. Conversely, if you're at a campus that lacks diversity, look for opportunities to engage with diverse audiences by participating in activities that may be outside your comfort zone. Your extra effort will yield rewards later.

- **Working on a project with a team will take more time but will produce a better project than an individual effort.** You may encounter difficult team situations that make you wonder if it would be easier to do the project on your own. In the long run, though,

a project that's been developed by a team tends to be a better project than one that comes from an individual effort. That's why so many companies and other organizations use teams to accomplish their objectives.

- **The most common mistake that people make in conflict resolution is bringing other people into the conflict too early.** People tend to want to talk about a problem with everyone but the person they have the problem with. Bringing in others will only complicate the problem and escalate the conflict. Once you have identified the problem (the first step), take time to have a conversation, one on one, with the person you're having the conflict with. It may be a tough conversation, but it will be worth having.

After you have defined the problem, your next step is to discuss the problem with the other person directly. If the problem is with your instructor, make an appointment during office hours to discuss the issue. If the conflict is with a classmate, set up a time to discuss the issue one on one and without interruptions or distractions. If you are emotional—angry, upset, or nervous—wait until you have calmed down to discuss the problem with the individual.

For conflict resolution to work, you must complete these first two steps. If you aren't satisfied with the result or you feel the problem has gotten worse, not better, then move to the next step: bringing others into the situation to help resolve it. If your conflict is with a professor, bring in the department chair or dean. If your conflict is with a roommate, bring your other roommates into the conversation. Again, your goal in this step is to resolve the issue. Stay focused on the specific problem that you defined in the first step, and try to maintain a calm, respectful attitude as you work through the conflict.

If your efforts to resolve a conflict with your professor are unsuccessful, even after consulting with the department head or dean, then ask to meet with the dean of students or the vice president for academic affairs. Only request this meeting if your earlier attempts at conflict resolution haven't worked. Don't start at the top. Doing so will only delay resolution.

Also keep in mind these tips for conflict resolution:

- Identify the problem and take ownership and responsibility for anything you did to contribute to it.
- Begin at the lowest level of conflict. Talk directly to the person you have the conflict with.
- If you can't resolve the conflict at the lowest level, then bring it to the next level:
    - Individual team member → Entire team → Professor
    - Professor → Department head → Dean
    - Roommate → Other roommates → Resident advisor (if in a dorm)
    - Coworker → Supervisor
- If the conflict needs to be brought to a higher level, document as much as you can in writing.
- Review your university's student code of conduct and other formal policies and procedures to learn about established approaches to conflict resolution.

CASE SCENARIOS

1. Jonathan was raised in a very religious household. He believes that homosexuality is wrong, and he is struggling with an assignment in one of his classes in which he must write about the issue from a sociological perspective. The professor cautioned students about the need to be objective in their papers, but Jonathan doesn't think he can. He decides to write an argumentative paper condemning homosexuality, and he uses both unscholarly sociological research and religious doctrines to support his arguments.

   Use the following scale to rate the decision that has been made (1 = Poor Decision, 5 = Excellent Decision). Be prepared to explain your answer.

   Poor Decision ← 1 ——— 2 ——— 3 ——— 4 ——— 5 → Excellent Decision

2. Marie has been married for 14 years, and she and her husband have twin 12-year-old girls. Since Marie started college two years ago, she's noticed that her husband seems less interested in her and what she's learning. In addition, he's started making fun of her desire to earn a degree. At first, Marie's husband encouraged her to enroll at the branch of the state university in their town, but now he seems to be against her continuing her education. Marie is discouraged by his reaction and has decided not to enroll next semester. In fact, she has missed the deadline for continuing students to register and to apply for financial aid.

   Use the following scale to rate the decision that has been made (1 = Poor Decision, 5 = Excellent Decision). Be prepared to explain your answer.

   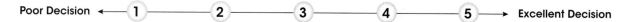

   Poor Decision ← 1 ——— 2 ——— 3 ——— 4 ——— 5 → Excellent Decision

3. One of Willis's professors has missed three night classes in a row without telling the students in advance and without providing a plan to make up the missed material. Willis really needs this class to complete his major in business, and he's worried that he won't be successful in later classes if he doesn't learn the content of this class. He's also worried that if he complains to the instructor, the instructor will lower his grade in retaliation. Willis decides to stick it out. He won't complain about the course, and he'll hope to earn a grade that's good enough to pass.

   Use the following scale to rate the decision that has been made (1 = Poor Decision, 5 = Excellent Decision). Be prepared to explain your answer.

   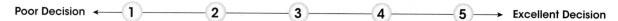

   Poor Decision ← 1 ——— 2 ——— 3 ——— 4 ——— 5 → Excellent Decision

Take It with You

Action Item	Deadline	First Step
Practice answering the questions "Who?" "What?" "How?" and "Why?" before communicating with someone.		
Identify the kinds of diversity (such as racial, socioeconomic) that are represented on your campus.		
Apply the tips for effective teamwork during your next team project.		
Follow the steps of effective conflict resolution to resolve your next conflict.		

REFERENCES

Cloud, H. & Townsend, J. (1992). *Boundaries: When to say yes, when to say no to take control of your life*. Grand Rapids, MI: Zondervan.

Payne, R.K., DeVol, P., & Smith, T. D. (2000). *Bridges out of poverty*. Highlands, TX: Aha!Process.

Zemke, R., Raines, C., & Filipczak, B. (2000). *Generations at work: Managing the clash of veterans, boomers, xers, and nexters in your workplace*. New York, NY: Amacom.

10 Information Literacy

"A 15-page research paper and a five-minute PowerPoint presentation. Both due during the las week of class," Juanita repeated to her mother over the phone.

"What topic do you have to write on?" her mother asked.

"We get to pick from a list," Juanita answered, looking over the list again, "but I don't even know what some of these topics are—like conflict management theory. I guess that's the point of doing research."

"You'd better get started, Juanita," her mother suggested. "I know how you are about writing papers—even when you end up doing well."

Juanita remembered how many nights she had stayed up writing papers at the last minute because she hadn't known for sure how to get started. She'd also convinced herself that she did better during the rush and with the excitement of the clock ticking.

"I guess this is my chance to break my bad habits," Juanita said. "Michael told me that Dr. Kirsey is tough on grading."

"I thought this was sociology, not English," her mother said.

"It is, Mom, but all of my instructors still expect me to write good papers. Most of them have PhDs! If this paper is not written well and does not have information from the right kinds of resources, then I can kiss a good grade goodbye," Juanita said. "And it's not just a paper. I have to get up and say something about what I learned."

"You're a good writer, Juanita. You've always loved to write," her mother reminded her. Juanita could hear the sound of running water in the background—a sign her mother was cleaning up the kitchen.

Juanita could not wait to find out more about possible topics for the project, so she decided to get a head start on the research by going to the library and browsing for ideas. Waiting for her professor to give her more information would make her nervous

Like Juanita, you'll be expected to handle a lot of different kinds of information about a variety of topics when you're in college. To support your success in that effort, this chapter will help you to do the following:

- Appreciate the importance of information literacy.
- Identify appropriate sources of information.
- Evaluate information for its reliability, credibility, currency, and accuracy.
- Use ideas and information ethically.

LEARNING OUTCOME

Evaluate sources for reliability, credibility, currency, and accuracy.

INFORMATION LITERACY PREPARES YOU FOR SUCCESS

As your college experience kicks into high gear, one of the many adjustments you'll have to face is the dramatic increase in the amount of information you need to process. Whether you are a part- or full-time student, you'll attend classes in which professors will present and review a lot of information, you'll have reading and research assignments for several classes at the same time, you'll process information about your degree plan and eventually your career plan, and you'll handle information about financial aid, graduation requirements, and other topics that pertains to your college experience. This information will come to you in many forms: textbooks, articles, websites, emails, discussion boards, Podcasts, lectures, forums, Twitter feeds, Facebook posts, flyers, announcements, and so on.

Your ability to handle this information and to use it effectively to make decisions and to succeed in college will depend on your information literacy. *Information literacy* "is the set of skills needed to find, retrieve, analyze, and use information" (American Library Association, 2012). To become truly information literate, you need to become proficient at finding information, understanding and evaluating that information, and using it effectively to complete important assignments and to make important decisions. See Exhibit 1, which lists and gives examples of the skills that underlie information literacy. These skills will serve you well throughout your lifetime, not just in college.

As explained by the American Library Association Presidential Committee on Information Literacy (1989):

> Ultimately, information literate people are those who have learned how to learn. They know how to learn because they know how knowledge is organized, how to find information, and how to use information in such a way that others can learn from them. They are people prepared for lifelong learning, because they can always find the information needed for any task or decision at hand.

EXHIBIT 1 What Is Information Literacy?

Skill	Examples
Find	<ul><li>Navigating the library catalog system to locate a book</li><li>Using an Internet search engine to find sources</li><li>Referencing a book's index to find coverage of a topic</li></ul>
Retrieve	<ul><li>Checking out a book from the library or photocopying pages</li><li>Downloading articles from the Internet and citing the source properly</li><li>Downloading statistical data from the U.S. Census</li></ul>
Analyze	<ul><li>Using three different sources by three different authors to support the same conclusion</li><li>Applying statistical analysis to data to show important patterns</li><li>Critiquing an expert's opinion because of weaknesses in his or her argument</li></ul>
Use	<ul><li>Making recommendations to a business owner based on your research findings</li><li>Making a financial decision of your own based on careful research</li><li>Using research to make a decision about how to vote during the next election</li></ul>

KNOW DIFFERENT WAYS TO FIND APPROPRIATE SOURCES

As noted, a lot of potential sources of information are available for your use in assignments and activities. That information might be in electronic form, available in print, or presented orally. Some information is already available and just needs to be located, while other information needs to be generated, such as an interview with an expert on a particular topic.

To avoid getting overwhelmed with the number and variety of potential sources of information, start with the specific assignment, project, or decision at hand. For example, if your purpose for gathering information is to write a research paper, then read the syllabus and assignment carefully and talk with your professor about his or her expectations. Your assignment and topic will influence what kinds of sources you will use for your paper.

Suppose your education class requires you to find websites that provide information on cyberbullying in elementary schools. For this assignment, you'll know that you can restrict your search to websites to gather information for your paper. However, if the same class requires you to write a research paper on the latest studies on cyberbullying, then you'll most likely use multiple sources, including scholarly articles in journals (accessed via your library's databases) and school and scholarly websites.

Prepare for a writing assignment by thinking about what you need and want to write about and what sources you will need to use.

Some professors provide specific, detailed guidelines for the types of sources they expect students to use, while others offer only vague instructions. In the latter case, try to spend time with the professor during office hours to clarify the kinds of information he or she recommends, especially if it's the first assignment you're completing for this professor.

If you're gathering information to help you make a decision, such as whether to take out a student loan, ask yourself what information would really help you decide. Perhaps you've seen movies such as *Mission Impossible*, in which special agents use computers and other high-tech gadgets to acquire information instantaneously to help them complete their missions. Imagine, for a moment, that you have that kind of access to information. What would you want to have in front of you to help you make an informed decision? Ideally, that information would help you identify all of your alternatives, the tradeoffs of each alternative, and the likelihood of success if you choose one alternative over another.

Once you have a good idea of the kinds of information you should use for your assignment or decision, then you can begin to identify and evaluate potential sources. It's at this point in the research process that many of your peers will instinctively jump on the Internet and start to use Google or another search

It's in the SYLLABUS

Information about writing expectations for your class can be found in the course outline, assignments, or grading sections of the syllabus. Consider these questions:

■ What are the expectations for writing assignments in your class?

■ Does the syllabus outline these expectations or provide grading criteria?

■ If you are unclear about the expectations for writing in your classes, how can you find out more information? What resources are available to help you determine what to expect?

engine to find sources of information. Although this strategy may be useful in some cases, it will rarely be your best option, so try to avoid following others who use this approach.

Instead, consider the following sources of information based on their potential usefulness, relevance, and reliability:

- *Consult library research guides and directories.* Start by consulting your campus library, either in person or via the website, to see if it offers research guides or directories that list various sources of information. Exhibit 2 shows a sample research guide from a college librarian that would serve as a useful starting point for any research project related to marketing.

- *Identify specific sources in advance.* Determine what information you would like to have to help you write a paper or complete a project. Would financial data, statistics, or other numeric information be most helpful, or do you need authoritative opinions or explanations of certain concepts or ideas? Your library will have specific sources that relate to both types of information. Knowing what you want in advance will aid your search.

- *Look for peer-reviewed sources.* If possible, use library databases to locate peer-reviewed sources of information about your topic, such as academic and scientific journal articles. When an article has been peer reviewed, the author's work has been carefully examined, challenged, and supported by other experts in the field. These high-level sources may be difficult to understand, but their summaries might indicate their potential usefulness for your assignment. The primary benefit of using peer-reviewed sources is that they provide information with a high level of credibility because of the scientific methods used to conduct the research and the reputations of the experts who write and review the articles.

- *Consult government sources.* Government agencies, such as the U.S. Bureau of Labor Statistics (www.bls.gov) and the U.S. Census Bureau (www.census.gov) provide a wealth of data and information about a wide variety of topics. When you use data from these sources, you provide authoritative support for your findings and opinions. After you locate useful data and information, be sure to take careful notes about the sources so that you can list them in an accurate bibliography.

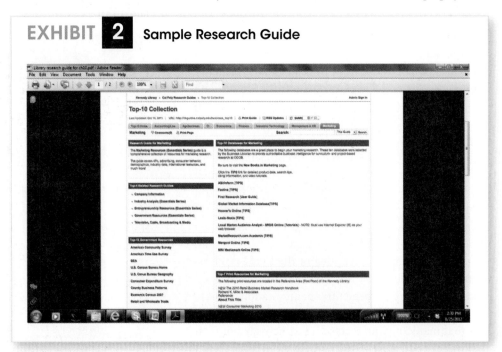

EXHIBIT 2 Sample Research Guide

Source: Mark Bieraugel, Robert E. Kennedy Library, Cal Poly.

- *Consult popular but credible publications.* Look for journals, magazines, and newspapers that are well known and widely read, such as the *New York Times,* the *Wall Street Journal, Time,* and *National Geographic,* just to name a few. Articles from these sources will be easier to read and understand than those in academic and scientific journals, but they will still provide a high level of credibility because of the established reputations of these publications.

- *Use credible websites.* Websites are obviously useful sources of information about many topics. Even so, always look for evidence of a specific authoritative organization or author that you can reference as the source of the information.

- *Generate your own information.* Depending on the project and your professor's requirements, you may also need to generate your own information or data. For example, you may need or want to interview experts on particular topics to gather their expert opinions and experiences. Or if you need numerical data, you may need to conduct your own study, such as comparing the prices of groceries across several supermarkets.

Because there are so many potential sources and types of information, it's best to seek guidance and clarification from your professor before beginning your research project. Finding authoritative sources of information and data that support your argument or thesis will greatly improve the quality of your work and, ultimately, your grade.

USE SOURCES THAT ARE RELIABLE, CREDIBLE, CURRENT, AND ACCURATE

After locating sources, spend time deciding if they are useful for your project. Good sources are reliable, credible, current, and accurate.

Again, look to your assignment and your professor for guidance if you are unsure whether a source is acceptable. Most likely, if you found the source in the library's catalog or databases, then it's credible.

Use Your Sources to Support Your Argument or Thesis

Once you've located sources that provide reliable and relevant information, use them to strengthen and support your argument or thesis. A research paper is different from an essay: Whereas an essay relies primarily on your own opinions, a research paper draws on outside sources to support your main idea.

What types of advertisements and news articles do you believe are the most persuasive? Chances are, you consider those that use factual data, expert sources, and logical arguments to support their point to be particularly persuasive. The same approach applies to your research paper. If the purpose of your paper is to argue a point, to make a recommendation, or to critically evaluate a theory or philosophy, then your paper will have a stronger argument if you can support it with verifiable facts and outside sources.

After you've written a first draft of your research paper, review it carefully. Use a highlighter to mark every statement

Writing is a process that takes time.

you make that someone might argue against or any claim you make that someone might doubt. Then consider whether you can find an outside source to support that argument or claim. For example, if you are writing a report about the effects of the 2010 British Petroleum (BP) oil spill on the economy of the U.S. Gulf Coast, you would provide economic data and quotes from industry experts to support your claims that the oil spill caused negative effects. Your research paper will be a better paper if you can provide research support for most, if not all, of your claims.

Evaluate Your Sources Carefully

So, you've located several sources of information and reviewed the information provided by each source. Next, it's a good idea to take time to evaluate the information for its reliability, credibility, currency, and accuracy:

- *Reliability:* Sources that are reliable are consistent over time. A tape measure, for example, provides a reliable measure of length every time you use it. In contrast, the commentary on TV news channels about a breaking news story might change rapidly as new information emerges. Blogs, Twitter feeds, Facebook posts, and other social media are often quite informative in covering fast-moving stories, but they are as reliable as other sources of information that remain consistent over time.
- *Credibility:* Is the author or source of the information an authoritative expert on this topic? What is his or her occupation, title, or background? Has the author written and published a lot of articles about this topic?
- *Currency:* How recent is the information? If you're writing a paper about the Civil War, it's quite acceptable to use sources of information that are quite old. If you're writing a paper about genetically modified crops, however, you'll want to draw information from sources that were published within the last few years.
- *Accuracy:* The best way to judge the accuracy of information from one source or article is to locate other sources that provide similar information. If two or more

THE UNWRITTEN RULES
Of Information Literacy

- **Most of your classmates will fall for the "Google trap."** Don't be one of them! You can distinguish yourself as an exceptional student by demonstrating an ability and willingness to search for sources of information that aren't retrieved from a Google search.

- **Information literacy is a great skill to emphasize in job interviews.** If you're interviewing for a part-time job, internship, or your full-time career, set yourself apart by demonstrating your ability to find, analyze, evaluate, and use information. Every job and every career requires having some level of information literacy.

- **You may encounter some tricky situations when you critically evaluate information.** In some situations, your professor might present information in a lecture that you later discover is either outdated or factually incorrect. Before you bring such an error to your professor's attention, make sure you have authoritative sources of information to back up your observation, and then schedule time to meet with the professor during office hours. Don't attempt to correct the professor publicly in class.

- **Quality trumps quantity.** Unless your professor has specific guidelines for the number of sources you should use, you will be better served if you find a few high-quality sources of information versus a lengthy list of unreliable sources.

- **Use direct quotes sparingly.** Direct quotes are your "nuclear" option, so to speak. Use them only when you don't think you can possibly paraphrase what the person is saying or a statement is particularly well expressed or well known. Otherwise, paraphrase the information and cite the source. Papers that are full of direct quotes suggest that the author can't think for himself or herself.

sources provide similar data or information, you can have greater confidence in the accuracy of the information.

To evaluate each source of information is a demonstration of your critical-thinking skills. It means that you've taken the time to consider whether information is reliable, credible, current, and accurate before using it to make a decision, reach a conclusion, or support an argument. The ability to think critically about the information you receive and use in college will serve you for a lifetime.

USE SOURCES ETHICALLY

When you find a source that you plan to use in your paper, record the details of publication for that source. How you do this will depend on the documentation style that your professor requires. The *documentation style* is the format in which you credit sources within the text of your paper and at the end in the References or Works Cited page of your paper.

Regardless of which style you use, incorporating sources into your paper requires that you provide essential information (usually the author's name and the title of the source) whenever you use it in your paper. Whether you are quoting directly from a source or paraphrasing information (that is, putting the author's ideas into your own words), you must let your readers know where the information came from. Proper acknowledgment and documentation are essential to incorporating sources correctly. Your professor will certainly want to hear your thoughts on the topic, but he or she will also expect you to find sources to support your ideas and then document them properly.

Be Sure to Avoid Plagiarism

Plagiarism is the act of using someone else's words, images, and ideas without properly and accurately acknowledging him or her. This definition can also apply to using artwork and computer programming code without acknowledgment.

Basically, any material that you use within an assignment (excluding information considered common knowledge) must be properly and accurately acknowledged. That means you must be familiar with and use the correct documentation style that your professor requires. Common documentation styles include MLA (Modern Language Association), APA (American Psychological Association), and CBE (Council of Biology Editors). The *Chicago Manual of Style* (CMS) also describes several documentation styles. Your library will have information that can help you use these styles accurately, and several websites provide information, as well. One such site is that of the American Library Association (www.ala.org).

Any time that you create, write, or produce an assignment, either as an individual or as part of a group, you'll need to document the information and sources you use. If your professor wants the assignment to be completely original—without the use of

Do your own work on papers and cite all sources you use in your writing.

INTEGRITY *Matters*

You should never copy answers that another student has written on your paper. Just as you would not share answers during a test, don't share your answers on work that's assigned out of class. If you have taken a class in a previous semester, also keep your assignments from being shared. Instructors may use the same assignments from semester to semester, and you don't want to put a fellow student in an awkward or potentially bad situation by sharing your work from a previous class.

YOUR TURN

In approximately 250 words, explain how students can compromise academic integrity, perhaps without even knowing it. Then describe what safeguards students can put in place to ensure academic integrity when working with others, whether fellow students or tutors.

sources—then you will need to adhere to those guidelines. If you are completing an assignment as part of a group, you may be asked to document which group members completed which parts of the assignment.

The following is a list of specific instances of plagiarism to avoid in all of your assignments:

- Buying or downloading a free paper off the Internet and turning it in as your own
- Copying and pasting material from an online or print source without acknowledging or properly documenting the source
- Allowing someone else to write all or part of your paper
- Creating a "patchwork" of unacknowledged material in your paper by copying words, sentences, or paragraphs from someone else and changing only small parts of the text
- Including fictitious references in your paper

When it comes to avoiding plagiarism, the simplest rule to remember is that if you had to look up the information or if you used a part or the whole of someone else's idea, image, or exact words, then you must let your professor and readers know. Like you would in any other unclear situation, ask for clarification. Your professor will be able to help you determine what you need to do if you are unsure.

Meeting EXPECTATIONS

The college will expect that I ...	To meet that expectation, I will ...
Example: . . . *use information ethically in my papers and presentations.*	Example: . . . *acknowledge all the sources of information I have used.*

CASE STUDIES

1. Renée is barely passing her literature class. She hasn't done well on the tests or the writing assignments, so she's asked someone to help her write her final literary analysis paper. Anne, a friend of her mother, has offered to help Renée write her paper, and when Anne meets with Renée, she offers to write down all of Renée's ideas, to organize them, and to reword all her sentences. Renée ends up getting an A on the paper—something that she hasn't been able to achieve all semester. She is thrilled that she has finally has received a good grade.

   Use the following scale to rate the decision that has been made (1 = Poor Decision, 5 = Excellent Decision). Be prepared to explain your answer.

   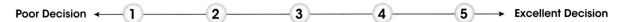

2. Paul is having a hard time understanding the research assignment that his government professor handed out to the class. He's had two months to work on the paper, but he hasn't done anything yet, and now he has only two weeks. Paul has decided to make an appointment with his professor before beginning the assignment, but he can't get in to see her until the end of the week. That means he'll lose four more days of working on the paper. Nonetheless, Paul is determined to start off right, and he's afraid that if he starts working on the paper before speaking to his professor, he'll get confused and end up feeling as though he wasted time.

   Use the following scale to rate the decision that has been made (1 = Poor Decision, 5 = Excellent Decision). Be prepared to explain your answer.

   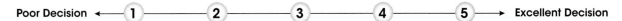

3. Pietra is afraid of public speaking and has postponed taking her speech class until her last semester in college. Now that she has enrolled, she feels that familiar fear and can't seem to shake it. The professor has lectured about overcoming speaking anxiety, and Pietra has read about this topic in her textbook. Even so, she doesn't think that she will be able to pass the class. She is supposed to give her first speech tomorrow and thinks that if she tells her professor she is sick, she can make up the assignment outside class, where no one can see her mess up. Even if her professor doesn't let her make up the missed speech, she thinks, she can just work really hard to make sure she still passes the class.

   Use the following scale to rate the decision that has been made (1 = Poor Decision, 5 = Excellent Decision). Be prepared to explain your answer.

Take It with You

Action Item	Deadline	First Step
Schedule an appointment with a university librarian or other staff member to learn about the resources available at your campus library.	_____	
Identify the projects in each of your courses that will require some form of research.	_____	
Determine which documentation style each of your professors prefers or requires.	_____	
	_____	

REFERENCES

American Library Association. (2012). Information literacy. Retrieved from http://www.ala.org/acrl/issues/infolit/overview/intro

American Library Association Presidential Committee on Information Literacy. (1989, January 10). Retrieved from http://www.ala.org/acrl/issues/infolit/overview/intro

11 Managing Stress

Evan is a student by day and a kick boxer by night, usually competing several times a semester. Sometimes, he wonders if he can do both and be successful in and out of the ring. A few years ago, he saw a doctor because of depression, and lately, he's started to feel the symptoms creeping up on him again.

"Evan, man, you're a little late today," his coach said. "What gives? You are usually early to practice."

"I had too much homework to do," Evan replied.

"Evan, I know you are committed to college," continued the coach. "That's great, but you have to do your time at the gym."

The words stung Evan! He was highly competitive and proud of his athletic ability, even though he had started to pack on the pounds from too much studying and poor eating.

Then, there was college—another goal that he wanted to achieve. When he registered for college, he really thought he could do both kick boxing and college and succeed at both.

Evan packed his sweatshirt into his gym bag, did his stretches, and thought about the homework he still had to finish before going to bed, which was usually about 2:00 A.M. After working out, he stopped on the way home to buy a few energy drinks and a protein bar, which would fuel him through completing his homework.

Evan's situation isn't unique. Every college student faces some form of pressure or stress. In an effort to help you successfully navigate these challenges, this chapter will enable you to do the following:

■ Recognize major stressors that affect students.
■ Understand your reaction to personal stressors.
■ Explore techniques for managing stress.
■ Develop strategies for maintaining your physical health.

LEARNING OUTCOME

Create a stress-management plan.

MyStudentSuccessLab (www.mystudentsuccesslab.com) is an online solution designed to help you 'Start strong, Finish stronger' by building skills for ongoing personal and professional development.

COLLEGE HAS STRESSORS ALL ITS OWN

College offers a lot of new experiences and opportunities, which can be fun and exciting but also stressful. *Stress* is a physical and psychological response to outside stimuli. In other words, just about anything that stimulates you can cause stress.

Not all stress is bad for you, however. For example, the stress you feel when you see someone get seriously hurt enables you to spring into action to help. For some students, the stress of an upcoming exam gives them the energy and focus to study. Without feeling a little stressed, these students might not feel the need to study at all. In fact, scientific research demonstrates that moderate levels of anxiety enhance performance compared to no anxiety at all, but too much anxiety can be harmful. In other words, a little bit of stress may be good, but too much is not. The key, then, is to manage stress well so it's not overwhelming.

The first step in developing a successful approach for managing stress in college is to identify and anticipate the circumstances and issues in your life that have the potential to cause stress. The acronym HALT, which stands for hungry–angry–lonely–tired, can help you anticipate when you might be less resilient to stressful situations. Suppose that you're waiting in line at the bank and you're hungry. You may be more irritable and impatient than if you had just enjoyed a good lunch or were sipping on your favorite coffee while in line.

Being aware of times and situations that cause you the most stress is one step toward helping manage stress better. In Exhibit 1, indicate whether each situation is or isn't stressful for you. Also consider other situations or people that cause you to react negatively.

By understanding the various factors and circumstances in your life that can trigger stress, you can develop an effective stress-management plan. The next step is to better understand how you tend to react to these stressors.

EXHIBIT 1   How Stressful Is This Situation?

Situation	Stresses Me	Does Not Stress Me
Starting a big project		
Paying bills		
Being in a messy environment		
Getting back graded papers and exams		
Not getting enough sleep		
Taking a personal or professional risk		
Getting out of bed in the morning		
Not getting feedback on my work		
Being distracted by other people		
Thinking about the future		
Taking tests		

Meeting EXPECTATIONS

The college will expect that I . . .	To meet that expectation, I will . . .
Example: . . . *manage my stress in healthy ways.*	Example: . . . *take advantage of college resources to help me maintain my health.*

KNOWING HOW YOU REACT TO STRESS CAN HELP YOU MANAGE IT

Not everyone handles stress the same way, and what is a stressful situation for you may not be for someone else. How you handle stress depends on your genetic makeup, your past experiences, and the stress-reducing techniques that you know and practice.

When you feel a lot of stress, how do you react?

Exhibit 2 lists some common types of reactions to stress—some healthy, some unhealthy. Review the list and use it to evaluate your reactions to common stressors. This list isn't intended to be complete, so you may react to stress in ways that aren't mentioned here.

The important point at this stage in developing a stress-management plan is to know yourself well enough to know (or to ask others who know you well) how you tend to react to stressful situations. Some of your reactions may be both helpful and healthy—for example, exercising and spending social time with others talking about your stress. Some of your reactions may be unhelpful and harmful to your health—for example, any forms of substance abuse. These kinds of responses will lead to even greater problems in your life and could seriously harm you.

To make sure you're on track with your stress-management plan, review the following tips for managing stress effectively.

We all sometimes feel overwhelmed by what we have to accomplish.

YOU CAN MANAGE YOUR STRESS

No doubt, you have felt stress since enrolling in college. You wouldn't be human if you didn't at least worry at the beginning of the semester how you will manage it all—family, work, college, and a personal life. Feeling stress is normal, but for college students, it can seriously derail them from achieving their goals if they can't manage it successfully. Looking for ways to minimize stress, not to eliminate it completely (because you can't!), and to maximize balance in your life will make your college experience more enjoyable and successful. See Exhibit 3 for a list of techniques for minimizing stress.

INTEGRITY *Matters*

Have you ever promised someone that you would do something for him or her, only to break your promise? No matter why we break a promise, we always feel some stress because our action or inaction can damage our relationships with others.

One way to eliminate stress and anxiety is to make integrity a top priority in your life. Promise only what you know you can deliver, and not only will your stress level go down, but you'll also feel good about maintaining your integrity.

YOUR TURN

In approximately 250 words, describe a time that you let someone down by not delivering on a promise. Discuss how you felt about not honoring your word and how your relationship ultimately changed with this person.

EXHIBIT 2 Evaluating Reactions to Stressors

As you review the following list, take a moment to evaluate how often you react to stressors in this way and whether this type of reaction is healthy and helpful.

Reaction to Stressor	How Often Do You React This Way?			Is This Reaction Healthy and Helpful?	
	Never	Sometimes	Always	Yes	No
Talking to others, or "venting," about a stressful situation, sometimes through Facebook posts or Twitter tweets					
Yelling or screaming about the person, situation, or circumstance that is causing the stress					
Going for a walk, practicing yoga, or doing some other form of exercise					
Arguing with others, insulting them, or criticizing them in an effort to "blow off steam"					
Writing in a journal about the experience and the stress and reflecting on why it's triggering such a reaction for you and what caused the stressful circumstance in the first place					
Drinking alcohol or taking drugs					
Praying, meditating, or engaging in some form of spiritual or religious expression					
Eating					
Sleeping					
Escaping from the stressor by going to a movie, listening to music, watching TV, or surfing the Web					
Engaging in artistic expression, such as art, music, dance, theater, or graphic design					

EXHIBIT 3 Techniques for Managing Stress

Practice deep breathing and yoga.	Maintain lines of communication.
Visualize a relaxing place and time.	Maintain flexibility and margin in your schedule and relationships.
Engage in physical activity.	Seek help if it becomes overwhelming.
Find activities that make you laugh.	Comfort yourself with familiar favorites.

Disarm the Negative Effects of Stress

Because you can't eliminate all stress, you'll need to develop methods for reducing the negative effects that your body and mind experience when you are stressed out. One of the quickest, easiest ways to reduce the negative effects of stress is to take a deep breath. You may have even told someone who was upset to breathe deeply in order to calm down. As many cultures have known for thousands of years, breath is an important part of life. For example, in yoga, the ability to control the breath is essential to controlling the mind and body and to bringing fresh air to the lungs and other organs.

Visualization is another method for reducing the effects of stress on the mind and body. To visualize a more relaxed time and place, all you need to do is find a quiet, comfortable spot, sit down, and close your eyes. Relaxation experts suggest that you visualize a place that makes you feel warm and relaxed. Many people think about a beach, because the mood there is often relaxed and the sound of the ocean is comforting. Try to find your own special place.

THE UNWRITTEN RULES
Of Managing Stress

- **All college students are under some kind of stress; they just handle it differently.** Students tend to think only about the stress they face, but the professors, staff members, and administrators on campus are also trying to manage stress. Everyone on campus has a shared responsibility to help each other manage stress and to try to avoid contributing to the stress that others experience.

- **Your choice of peers will dramatically affect how stressful your life is and how well you manage stress.** Face it: Some people just seem to create more drama and stress than others. It might be funny and entertaining for a while, but after a time, it can wear on you and actually draw you in. Steer clear of "drama queens" and "drama kings," and spend time with people who have healthy outlets for stress, such as laughing, exercising, and engaging in healthy and enjoyable recreational activities.

- **Maintaining good physical health in college requires more discipline than in your younger years.** You won't always feel like exercising, so at times, you'll have to just gut it out and go to the gym. You'll also be tempted to eat sugary snacks and drink sodas versus having a nutritious meal and a healthy beverage. Try to make good choices more often than you make poor ones. The reality is that your body becomes less forgiving of your poor choices as you get older.

- **We need to help each other.** If you see a friend or classmate is clearly struggling, then reach out and support his or her efforts to get help. You don't have to be a counselor; just encourage and help the individual to get an appointment with a counselor. Wouldn't you want someone to do the same for you?

Find time to incorporate fun activities to help you manage your stress.

Once you decide where you want to go mentally, start noticing the details in your place. If you are at the beach, then you should feel the warmth of the sun. Next, listen to the waves crashing on the surf and smell the salty air. Depending on how long you need to visualize this special place, you may want to stick your toe in the water or lie down on the sand and soak up the rays—leaving your stress in those designated beach trash cans. In this method of relaxation, the goal is to stay in your place as long as you need to. When you return mentally to your present location, you should feel refreshed and renewed.

Sometimes, physical activity can be a better stress reliever than mental exercises. Getting outside or going to the gym to work out your frustrations and stress is an excellent way of maintaining your health. By exercising, you eliminate the physical side effects of stress while you take your mind off your troubles. If you don't usually exercise, take it slowly. Start with a 15-minute walk around the block, or do some simple stretching exercises on the floor. Overdoing exercise can lead to more stress, so start small and increase the time you spend getting your blood circulating as you get stronger.

If you happen to exercise too much, look to massage therapy to reduce your stress. Although massage is a little less conventional than other methods of reducing stress, it can improve circulation and alleviate muscle soreness. Seek professional massage therapy, or ask a family member to rub your neck, shoulders, or feet. Massage therapy can give you the rejuvenation you need to tackle the rest of the week.

You have likely heard the cliché that "Laughter is the best medicine," and it's also an ideal way to eliminate stress. Have you ever been in a stressful situation when someone made you laugh and you thought, "Boy, I needed that"? You probably felt all the tension melt away as you doubled over giggling. Surrounding yourself with people who make you laugh is one way to keep stress at a minimum. Other ways include renting comedies or reading funny books. Of course, good, old-fashioned acting silly can relieve stress and anxiety, as well.

In addition, you can comfort yourself with familiar favorites to eliminate the negative effects of stress. A special meal or a visit with your best friend can put you at ease. Looking at old photographs, reminiscing about family trips, and watching your favorite movies can be great stress relievers. If you have enrolled in college in a new town or you have moved out on your own for the first time, you may find comfort in the familiar, whether it's an old pillow or a favorite movie. Make sure, though, that your methods of reducing negative stress are healthy. Using drugs and alcohol may temporarily relieve stress, but they cause more problems in the long run.

Reducing the negative stress that you experience on the job, at home, and in college will be easier if the lines of communication are open and you are committed to explaining what is stressing you out. On the job, you may want to talk to your supervisor (rather than your coworkers, unless they can truly help) about what's causing you stress and how you can manage it. Your boss may be able to reassure you about the support you have as you juggle work and college. At home, you may want to talk with family members about what stresses you out and why. Explain that your college career is temporary and that the adjustments that are needed at home will most likely be temporary, too, until you complete your degree. If you are experiencing stress in college, speaking with a professor or a counselor can help you reduce the negative effects. Remember that the people who work at a university were once students, too, and they may have some good tips that helped them minimize stress when they were in college.

Being Flexible Can Help Minimize Stress

An important method of managing stress is to remain flexible. If you try to control too many aspects of your life, you'll quickly discover that you can't handle them all. Although it's important to manage your time and to mark your progress toward your goals, you still need to plan for the unexpected and to be willing to make adjustments.

> ## It's in the SYLLABUS
>
> Review your course syllabi to determine what you will need to be aware of during the semester to better manage your stress. Also consider these questions:
>
> - What parts of the syllabi will cause you the most stress in terms of meeting professors' expectations?
> - What expectations will be easiest for you to meet?
> - If you find yourself overwhelmed or confused by the expectations in your courses, what can you do to help reduce your stress?

Good time managers plan for problems by keeping their schedules loose enough to make room for adjustments. For example, if you have a doctor's appointment at 2:00 P.M., you shouldn't schedule a job interview at 3:00 P.M. Delays in the doctor's office or traffic problems could keep you from your 3:00 appointment and cause more stress.

Instead, give yourself plenty of time in between scheduled tasks, especially if you have to rely on others' time-management skills. The idea is to allow some margin or leeway in your life so you can absorb the so-called unexpected events that come up (which you can actually come to expect). This margin can be in the form of time (giving yourself the extra minutes needed to handle a traffic jam or a full parking lot and still make it to class) or money (setting aside a certain amount each month for an emergency fund to cover the flat tires, lost books, and parking tickets that always seem to come out of nowhere).

You can also build margins in your relationships by having candid conversations with your friends, roommates, and loved ones about how you'll need their help and understanding when you're facing a lot of stress in your life. Simply forewarning your roommates that you have a challenging final exam next week can help them anticipate and effectively manage the situation if you seem more irritable or impatient than usual.

Seek Help If Stress Becomes Overwhelming

If you ever feel as though you can't cope with the amount of work and responsibility that you have, despite attempts to reduce your stress, then seek professional help. Excessive crying, difficulty breathing, inability to get out of bed, and suicidal thoughts are severe reactions to stress. Knowing when to reach out to other people will be crucial in your recovery.

When asking for help, find someone you trust and who will be objective about your experiences. Sometimes, a close friend or family member is your best ally, but other times, an outside party, who will listen to you without judging, can be extremely helpful.

Whoever you talk to, be honest about what you're feeling. Don't try to minimize your fear or anxiety. The more the person knows about what you're experiencing, the better able he or she will be to help. Most universities have professional counselors that you can meet with to share your experiences. They are professionally trained to help individuals navigate the stress and difficult emotional challenges that college students face, and they're on staff at the university to help you. Check with your health center or student affairs office if you can't locate contact information on the college website.

YOUR PHYSICAL HEALTH IS IMPORTANT, TOO

Making good food choices is the foundation for overall good health.

Your physical health directly affects your ability to perform well in college. Also, the habits you develop in college for maintaining your physical health will set the stage for your long-term health and well-being.

Nutrition Gives You Fuel

One key to living a healthy life is eating nutritious food. Getting the recommended daily allowances of fruits, vegetables, whole grains, proteins, and fats is a commonsense approach to healthy eating.

Eating healthy also means eating regularly. Most experts recommend eating smaller meals more frequently, rather than heavy meals five to seven hours apart. Start the day with a healthy breakfast, and you'll feel more alert and energized throughout the morning.

In addition to eating smaller, frequent, nutritious meals, drink plenty of water throughout the day. Doing so has numerous health benefits, including regulating body temperature and assisting digestion. Also consider drinking juices to get more nutrients (Zellman, 2011).

Exercise Gives You Energy and Relieves Stress

Exercising regularly can lower blood pressure, increase metabolism, improve muscle tone, and lessen the chance of developing a disease that is directly related to a sedentary lifestyle. It can also improve your mood and your self-confidence. Doing 30 minutes of sustained activity three or four times a week will provide you with many health benefits.

Sleep Recharges Your Batteries

Getting enough sleep each night is as important to maintaining good health as what you eat and how often you exercise. Experts say that an adult should get seven to nine hours of sleep a night to function normally throughout the day. Maintaining a regular schedule of going to bed and getting up will help you get the amount of sleep you need.

Pulling all-nighters to study for tests or to complete assignments is strongly discouraged. By not sleeping, you will be less likely to perform well the next day.

Drugs and Alcohol Can Quickly Derail Your Health and Life

The more educated you become about the health risks associated with smoking and using smokeless tobacco, the more clearly you will recognize that using tobacco products can cause serious health consequences. There are a variety of methods for quitting.

Take the time to investigate what methods your college and community offer to smokers and users of smokeless tobacco. Your college may provide information, support groups, or physician referrals for students who want to quit.

Alcohol and drugs are two other health issues that can dramatically affect college students. Whether these substances are consumed for recreational purposes or because of more serious health reasons (such as addiction), they are dangerous. Abusing drugs and alcohol should not be part of your college experience, because they will impede your achievement and potentially harm you and your loved ones.

Using medications for purposes other than for what they were prescribed can also have grave consequences, including death. Excessive use of medications that contain amphetamines and narcotics can lead to addiction and serious physical and emotional problems.

Yes, We Do Need to Talk about Sex

A discussion of health issues would not be complete without talking about sexual health. Most colleges and universities strive to educate their students—especially those who are recently out of high school—about sexual responsibility, sexual assault, and common sexually transmitted diseases (STDs). Risky behaviors, which include having sex with multiple partners and having unprotected sex, open the door to possible infections and illnesses, such as chlamydia, gonorrhea, genital herpes, HIV (human immunodeficiency virus), and AIDS (acquired immune deficiency syndrome).

Some diseases can be transmitted in ways other than sexual intercourse. Hepatitis B and C are both diseases that can be contracted through sharing razors and toothbrushes, as well as body piercing and tattooing.

Sexual assault in the university environment is a troubling phenomenon that shouldn't be ignored. Some of the most common incidents of sexual assault are related to excessive consumption of alcohol and date rape, which involves two people who actually know each other. The Rape, Abuse, and Incest National Network (RAINN) provides numerous resources that students can use to educate themselves about risks, consequences, and preventive actions.

Depression and Suicide Are Sad but Real Occurrences in College

Students' problems with depression often start before they enroll in college. Signs of depression include loss of pleasure in activities, feelings of hopelessness, inability to get out of bed, increased use of alcohol or drugs, changes in appetite or weight gain or loss, changes in sleep patterns (sleeping too little or too much), extreme sensitivity, excessive crying, lack of energy or interest in participating in activities, and lack of interest in taking care of oneself.

Suicide is another mental health issue that's associated with depression. Thoughts of ending your life should always be taken seriously, and you should seek help immediately. Call a college counselor, an advisor, a hospital emergency room, or 911 if you are thinking about committing suicide. If one of your friends or roommates exhibits any worrisome behaviors or says anything that suggests thoughts of suicide, do everything you can to put him or her in contact with a professional on campus or at the local hospital who can help.

CASE SCENARIOS

1. Vin-Singh has been having trouble sleeping since he started college. He shares an apartment with another student who likes to stay up late and play loud music. Vin-Singh eats well and avoids caffeinated drinks, but he doesn't exercise regularly and often feels anxious when he tries to sleep. He has a research paper due in one week, and in three days, he must take a final exam that's worth 50% of his overall grade. Because Vin-Singh hasn't been sleeping well, he feels overwhelmed by what he has left to do before the semester is over. A friend suggested that he get some power energy drinks and caplets to get through the last week and promised that once he finishes his final assignment, he will get back to feeling better. Vin-Singh gets the energy boosters and starts taking them.

   Use the following scale to rate the decision that has been made (1 = Poor Decision, 5 = Excellent Decision). Be prepared to explain your answer.

   Poor Decision ⟵ 1 ——— 2 ——— 3 ——— 4 ——— 5 ⟶ Excellent Decision

2. Wanda hasn't exercised since she was in high school, and now, 20 years later, she's realized the importance of improving her health. In fact, at 5 feet, 9 inches tall, she wonders if the 30 pounds she's gained since high school are keeping her from feeling her best as she juggles the demands of college. She is about to start her last year of college—one that will be stressful, as she takes classes that will help her pass a nursing licensing exam and get a good job. Wanda also wants to lose the weight and to start an aggressive exercise program. She's decided to start lifting weights three times a week, running four times a week, and restricting her caloric intake to 1,200 calories a day.

   Use the following scale to rate the decision that has been made (1 = Poor Decision, 5 = Excellent Decision). Be prepared to explain your answer.

   Poor Decision ⟵ 1 ——— 2 ——— 3 ——— 4 ——— 5 ⟶ Excellent Decision

3. Ever since D.J. started college, he's focused on his studies and has cut out all activities that don't help him achieve his educational goals. He's told his friends that he won't be able to hang out with them; he's cut back on his hours at work; he's stopped playing basketball and running; and he's even stopped attending religious services so he has time to take as many class hours as possible each semester. D.J. wants to graduate with a degree as soon as he can and then start working, and his grades are good. Although he has been feeling tired and depressed a lot lately, he believes that these feelings are short term and that he'll return to his routine after completing his degree. D.J. has 10 months left before he reaches his goal of graduating.

   Use the following scale to rate the decision that has been made (1 = Poor Decision, 5 = Excellent Decision). Be prepared to explain your answer.

   Poor Decision ⟵ 1 ——— 2 ——— 3 ——— 4 ——— 5 ⟶ Excellent Decision

Take It with You

Action Item	Deadline	First Step
Identify potential stressors in your life.		
Recognize how you typically respond to stress.		
Develop strategies for managing stress in college.		
Develop a plan of action for maintaining good physical health.		

REFERENCE

Zellman, K.M. (2011). 10 ways to lose weight without dieting: Simple changes to your lifestyle can help you lose weight and keep it off. *WebMD*. Retrieved from http://www.webmd.com/diet/features/10-ways-to-lose-weight-without-dieting

12 Career Exploration

A big, red arrow pointed to the ballroom. In it, dozens of booths invited students to leave their resumes and to learn more about a variety of local and national businesses and industries.

Fresh from class, in jeans and his old university sweatshirt, Evan stopped to pick up a company brochure.

"I'm planning on going to all the booths," he told Michael. "Are you?"

Michael, wearing khakis and a white shirt, had done a little research and had already decided on the two booths he wanted to visit.

"No," he said. "I plan on finding the two companies I checked out on the Internet last night, telling them what I know about the open positions, and leaving my resume."

"Aren't you afraid you'll be cutting yourself short? Shouldn't you hit every one of the booths, just in case?" Evan asked.

"I don't know," Michael replied. "I guess with all my time in the military, I have a lot of experience doing different jobs."

"But there are so many options," Evan continued.

"Well, what degree can you earn that will get you a job that pays well?" asked Michael.

"I'm not sure," Evan told him.

"You won't be landing any jobs like that the way you are dressed today!" Michael said, smiling at his friend.

Evan pulled out 30 copies of his resume from his backpack and walked to the first table and introduced himself.

"Hi, I'm Evan," he said to a woman representing an aeronautics firm. "It's a pleasure to meet you. So, tell me what your company does and what I would do if I worked for you."

Michael walked straight to one of the two health care companies at the fair to deliver his resume.

Like Evan and Michael, you will have the opportunity to pursue a full-time career after you graduate from college—a career that capitalizes on your talents and abilities. To prepare you for a successful career, this chapter will help you to do the following:

- Identify careers that relate to your interests.
- Develop strategies for exploring a career.
- Establish a plan for networking to enhance career exploration and growth.
- Write an effective resume.

LEARNING OUTCOME

Create a career exploration plan.

MyStudentSuccessLab (www.mystudentsuccesslab.com) is an online solution designed to help you 'Start strong, Finish stronger' by building skills for ongoing personal and professional development.

It's in the SYLLABUS

Your course syllabi may help you in your career exploration. Look at what you are covering during the semester in each class. Also consider these questions:

- Do any topics really interest you?

- Do you find yourself drawn to certain subjects? What are they?

- Which professors will be helpful to you in the future?

Whether you know exactly what career you want or are still exploring the possibilities, your college experience can help you focus on what you want out of your professional life. Although it may seem like your career won't start until you're done with college, the exciting reality is that the decisions you are making today are already starting to form your career.

College is the time for exploring and preparing for a career, and the first step is to know your goals and what values you want to uphold.

Career Values and Goals Set the Course for Your Journey

Before you begin delving into the resources and services available at your college, take some time to reflect on what your career values and goals are. *Values* are personal and professional qualities and principles that are deeply important to you. For example, you may have a passionate interest in working for a company that makes products or provides services that have a positive impact on society or the environment. Or it may be critically important for you to work for an organization that is honest and ethical.

In addition to considering your values as they relate to your career, you may also want to consider what your goals are. *Goals* are tangible outcomes that you want to achieve in your personal and professional lives. Perhaps one of your goals is to move up quickly in a company, to find a business that will allow you to indulge in one of your values, or to travel and meet a diverse group of people.

When you get to the point that you'll be creating clear, realistic, and reachable career goals, your values will inform what you write down or tell others. Your values and goals will also help you talk with a career counselor, search for employment, and interview for a job.

Different Careers Mean Different Experiences

In addition to your personal values and goals, consider what you value in a career and what kinds of experiences you want to have. For example, do you value working with others in projects with strict deadlines, or would you prefer to work alone with little supervision? Your answer to this question and others can help you determine what you value and what careers may work best for you. If, for instance, you have a strong interest in writing but you prefer working with others, you may decide to choose a career that has many opportunities for collaboration when writing.

If you aren't sure where to start when considering your career values and goals, then check out various career assessment programs, such as DISCOVER and Kuder, at your career counseling center. There are also a number of books, such as Bolles's (2011) *What Color Is Your Parachute?* and websites that offer guidance for identifying your career interests, even at the early stages of your college career.

The career landscape can seem daunting and complex, especially because technology seems to cause careers to change quickly. Careers that existed 10 years ago may not exist four years from now, and careers that didn't exist a few years ago are

Meeting EXPECTATIONS

The college will expect that I . . .	To meet that expectation, I will . . .
Example: . . . *know what career I want to pursue when I graduate.*	Example: . . . *explore my options and take a proactive role to determine which careers would be best for me.*

now emerging. For this reason, don't put pressure on yourself to identify a specific company and job title for your career goal. Instead, keep your focus on the kind of career you want in terms of its general characteristics: work environment, type of industry, technical requirements, individual versus team environment, highly structured versus unstructured organizational structure and job functions, and so forth. Take time to browse career listings on websites (such as career-builder.com), and save copies of the posts that capture your interest. Doing these things will help you paint a picture that captures both your values and goals as they emerge and develop over time.

It's OK if your interests change over time. That will happen as you take more classes and gain new perspectives from your college experience. In fact, in today's work environment, the average individual will have several careers over his or her lifetime. What you're developing in college is the ability to identify your interests and abilities and to match them with the career opportunities in the marketplace. You may not want to face this reality now, but you may very well find yourself back in college later in life to pursue an advanced degree or certificate or a second bachelor's degree as you re-create yourself throughout your lifetime. As you learn to use the tools and resources discussed in the next section, you'll be encouraged to know that they can serve you well throughout your career journey.

THERE ARE SEVERAL WAYS TO EXPLORE YOUR CAREER

Chances are, several resources and events are available on your campus to support your efforts to explore and pursue your career options and opportunities. These include career counselors and professors, career fairs, and internships.

Use events and people on campus as opportunities to help you build a professional network.

Career Counselors Can Be Your Best Supporters

Even though you won't pursue a full-time career until you graduate, commit yourself to meeting with a counselor your freshman year so you can put an effective plan in place for both internships and your career. Each college offers different services in its career center, but most provide access to interest inventories and resources on different careers, which can help you pinpoint which careers you are best suited for. In addition, career centers may offer help with writing a cover letter and resume and tips for interviewing for a job. Evan should spend some time in his college's career library to learn more about careers before he hits all of the employers at the career fair.

Don't forget that your professors can also be great career counselors. They often have connections with people in the field or have friends or relatives working in different industries. You never know when your sociology professor may have a contact at an accounting firm or your biology professor may have a connection with the human resources department at an advertising firm. Tell professors what you want to do as a career whenever you have a chance. They may be likely to remember you and your goals when they meet someone in your field of study.

Internships Give You and Your Employer a Chance for a "Test Drive"

Another work option for college students is an internship. An *internship* is a supervised position that allows a student to work for an organization before he or she graduates. Some internships are unpaid, which makes them less attractive to students who need to work. However, you may be able to earn academic credit for a paid or unpaid internship, so check with your advisor about this possibility well in advance.

Being an intern is a great way to make progress toward your degree and to explore a career at the same time. Another idea is to volunteer once or twice a week at a place of business. If you have a few extra hours a week or can trade college credit for an internship, then you should investigate the benefits of interning.

Why are internships such good opportunities for college students? One reason is that they allow you to work closely in a field that you may be interested in. In addition, being an intern can help you explore different ways that your major can be used in the workforce. For example, an English or journalism major may want to participate in an internship as a copywriter at a newspaper or as a technical editor at a publisher. A computer science major may want to intern at a small business to get practical experience with computer networking issues on a small scale. Opportunities like these can give you firsthand experience with using what you're learning in your degree.

Being an intern also allows you to network with others who can help you find a job once you graduate. Even if you decide that you don't want to work in the same area as your internship, you will have made contacts that may help you find a job in another field.

If you decide to intern, treat it as you would a job in your chosen career. Some employers rely on interns to complete certain projects each year, and they expect interns to be serious about the position, even if they don't get paid. Keeping a good attitude and being self-motivated are excellent ways to shine during your internship. In addition, be sure to meet regularly with your supervisor to ask questions and to get guidance on projects. Most of all, make the best of your unique opportunity, and add that experience to your resume.

NETWORKING OPENS DOORS FOR YOUR CAREER

Networking is defined as the "sharing of knowledge and contacts; getting the help you need when you need it from those from whom you need it . . . ; [and] building relationships before you need them" (Darling, 2010, p. 16). Now more than ever, networking is an essential part of an effective career search. If you ask 10 recent college graduates who have full-time careers how they landed their jobs, chances are that at least six of them will tell a story about how someone they knew helped them meet someone in the organization to get a first interview. If you establish good relationships with a variety of individuals across multiple companies and industries throughout your college experience—including your freshman year—then these individuals will become your primary gateway to getting initial interviews.

It's important to establish what networking can and cannot do for your career search. Effective networking throughout your college years can help you get your foot in the door at various organizations, and it may help you land that first interview. At that point, however, it's all up to you. Someone else's referral on your behalf is often enough for a recruiter to take time to give you an interview, but it's not enough for a recruiter to hire you. You have to prove yourself in the interview process, and after you've been hired, you have to prove yourself on the job.

In a competitive job market, in which hundreds of people are applying for a single position, landing that first interview is a crucial step. Networking can help you get there.

Networking Is More than Exchanging Business Cards

When you see the word *networking*, what scene or activity comes to mind? The stereotypical perception of networking is a bunch of people introducing themselves to each other and making small talk at a social or business function. Some people think they've

THE UNWRITTEN RULES

Of Career Planning

- **"The early bird gets the worm."** Maybe you haven't heard this phrase before. It means that someone who is first to pursue an opportunity has a better chance of seizing it. This holds true for your career pursuit, as well. If you are proactive and ahead of your peers in developing a resume, building a network, and applying for internships, then you'll give yourself a better chance of securing a good job, both while you're in college and after graduating.

- **The best careers come from where you least expect them.** While serving as a restaurant server or hostess, you might serve a client who turns out to be a major employer, recruiter, or entrepreneur. By demonstrating some interest in that person and listening well, you might pick up clues that open the door for you to introduce yourself and express interest in the company. Be ready to give your 30-second "elevator pitch" at any time—even in the bathroom!

- **Students can have business cards, too.** If you have access to a computer, then you have what you need to design and print a professional-looking business card. Include your name, the university you attend, your major, and your contact information. Be sure to have some of these cards with you at all times.

- **E-portfolios are coming.** An e-portfolio is a website where students compile carefully selected samples of their academic work and accomplishments to show to prospective employers and graduate schools. Increasingly, employers want to see more than just your resume. They want to see samples of your actual work, including papers you've written, computer programs you've developed, projects you've completed, and problems you've solved. If you start collecting and organizing your work immediately during your first term of college, then you'll have a lot more content to use for an e-portfolio when you're ready to build it.

done a good job of networking if they came home from an event with a lot of business cards in their pockets.

Networking is a lot more than that. It certainly begins with an initial point of contact, and for that, you need to make a professional first impression. How you dress, what you say, and how you act during the initial social exchange will be important. But once you've made that initial contact with someone, how you follow up and maintain contact with him or her really determines the value of your network.

Suppose that you're at a relative's wedding, and you meet someone who has a highly successful career at an accounting firm. At the time, you have no interest in accounting, nor do you know much about the company the individual works for. Even so, you take time to ask questions about the individual's career and organization, and you politely ask for his business card or contact information.

Was that networking? Yes, but you were just getting started! It's what happens after the introduction that matters most.

When you get home, you need to add that person's contact information to a database and then compose a follow-up email or personal letter. In it, express that you enjoyed meeting the individual and learning about his career, and say that you'd like to stay in touch as your college career progresses. If you have prepared a current resume, send it to the individual, even if you don't have a present interest in a career at his organization.

In the months and years to follow, use a calendar system to remind yourself to touch base with this person. Update him on your accomplishments in college, ask him about his career accomplishments, ask him questions about how he chose his career, arrange an informational interview at his firm, and share any news articles that you read that have something to do with his industry or company.

As you invest in this relationship over time, you'll build a connection that is far more extensive than what you had when you first met this person. Then, when you really need this individual and the others in your network to help you secure that first interview, they will know you well enough to trust in your personal qualities and professionalism.

When someone takes the risk of recommending you to a friend or associate for a job interview, that person is putting his or her own reputation at risk on your behalf. Asking for a recommendation is a significant request! Successful networking, over time, will establish a range of personal and professional relationships that can help you make the right connection at the right time when your career search gets into full swing.

If you wait until late in your college career to start networking, it will be far more difficult for you to prove your sincerity and professionalism through the test of time. Start networking early and build a broad network, because you never know where your interests may take you in the future.

Networking Face to Face

The most effective method of networking is to build relationships through face-to-face interactions. You can pursue a number of specific activities to help you form broad, long-term connections:

Practice interviewing with a fellow student or a career counselor before going out there for real.

- *Join clubs on campus that suit your interests.* Even if a club is not career related, such as a drama club, you will meet people who may be future contacts for jobs.

- *Scan your school newspaper and announcements for events, such as guest speakers and discussion panels.* Colleges often bring in influential experts and industry leaders for speaking engagements. Attend these events when you can, not only to learn new perspectives but also to try to meet these individuals and introduce yourself.
- *Join a college ambassador club or another host-related student organization.* Many colleges have a student ambassador group that plays a lead role in hosting distinguished college guests, provides campus tours for visitors, and represents the college at community events, such as chamber of commerce meetings and special task forces and committees.
- *Consider a student leadership position on your campus.* Student leaders, such as members of the student council, often have special access to college administrators and community leaders.
- *Get involved in community service and philanthropic activities.* Industry and community leaders—the kinds of people who are ideal for including in your personal network—are often actively engaged in nonprofit organizations, community service activities, and philanthropy. You probably won't bump into the chief executive officer (CEO) of a large company in your daily life as a college student, but if you invest in community service and philanthropy, you might find yourself working next to someone who could eventually become a valuable member of your network.

As you pursue networking opportunities, carry them out with a genuine interest in making a contribution to the organization; don't participate just to meet people. Before you commit to any club, organization, community event, or philanthropic cause, be sure that it's something you believe in and are willing to support. Otherwise, your lack of sincerity and commitment will affect your reputation, and you'll do more harm than good. However, if you get involved in something that you feel committed to, the personal network of relationships you establish will open doors in your career that you never could have imagined for yourself.

Networking Online

One of the largest trends in networking is using social networking websites, such as LinkedIn and Facebook, to create networks of friends, family, and special interest groups. The possibilities seem endless for ways to use the Internet to connect with others who have special interests and activities or problems to solve.

With that said, if you decide to join a network that focuses on an interest of yours, such as computer programming, be sure to investigate who runs the group, what kinds of information are shared, and how active the group is. Some networks will be more active than others, which will make it easier to connect with others and get involved. Other networks or groups may be less active, which won't help you if you are trying to get to know others as potential contacts in the future.

Because creating networks of your own is so easy, you may want to consider creating an interest group if you can't find one related to your career of interest. Networking sites such as Facebook allow you to set up groups that can be used for professional, educational, or social purposes.

If you decide to set up a profile on a social networking site such as LinkedIn, take time to establish a profile that is well written, professional, and informative. These sites often allow you to post a photo, so provide one that shows you dressed professionally, as you would appear for a job interview. Upload your entire resume or the content of the resume, and make sure that all of your contact information is current, accurate, and professional.

Social networking sites often have a mechanism for you to connect with others, and in most cases, doing this requires the other person to accept your invitation. Be sure to initiate such an invitation with a courteous, respectful approach, recognizing that if the other person chooses to connect with you, it's comparable to the risk he or she faces when recommending you to others. This isn't a trivial decision, so be sure that your profile and your request are presented in a manner that gives the other person confidence that you will represent yourself—and him or her—well.

YOUR RESUME ESTABLISHES YOUR PERSONAL BRAND

As you progress through your degree, your resume and cover letter will serve as a tangible representation of your personal brand—who you are, what you know, what you can do, and how you're different from your peers and other individuals competing for the same jobs. Just as McDonald's, Apple, and the Gap invest significant effort and resources to define themselves through distinctive brands, so you need to establish a distinctive personal brand that makes you recognizable and relevant to organizations that need a talented workforce.

If you'd like to learn more about developing your personal brand, consult Tim O'Brien's (2007) book *The Power of Personal Branding*. It's a great resource for this important topic (www.thepersonalbrandinggroup.com).

Your Resume Puts Your Life on Paper

Learning to write a resume is an essential skill for a new college graduate, and there is no time like the present to begin honing that skill. Your resume is no place to be modest, but neither is it a place to embellish or misrepresent your skills or experience. All individuals have something—whether it's the classes they've taken, the projects they've completed, or the hardships they've overcome in their personal lives—that makes them special and

INTEGRITY *Matters*

While you may be excited to list your accomplishments on your resume, you must be sure not to go overboard in describing what you have done. A good rule to follow is to always provide accurate, truthful information in your resume and cover letter. Highlight your accomplishments without exaggerating them.

Lying on a resume is called "resume padding," and it can get you in serious trouble. At the very least, if a prospective employer discovers what you've done, you might not get the job. At the very worst, you might get fired after you are hired if the company finds out that your resume contains false information.

YOUR TURN

In approximately 250 words, describe where you think the line exists between making your accomplishments noteworthy and exaggerating them. Discuss what steps you will take to ensure that all the information on your resume and cover letter is accurate.

that gives them the experience and personal qualities that are important to an employer. The challenge is to describe those qualities in a resume and to do it in no more than a page, for most job applications.

A number of university-affiliated websites provide guidance on how to develop an effective resume. Your university's career services office will offer support resources, as well.

To get started, here's a basic list of what your resume should include:

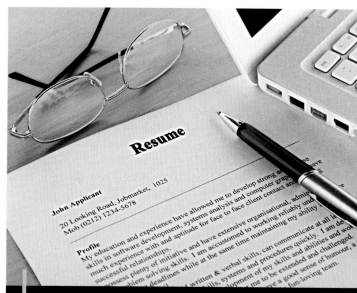

Creating a strong, compelling resume can be the difference between getting an interview and getting overlooked.

- *Your name and contact information, including your address, phone number, and email address:* Make sure your voicemail has an appropriate message on it and that your email is professional, as well. An address like ejcantu@abcmail.com is preferable to one like bananafreak72@chunkymonkey.com.

- *A clear objective or purpose statement that describes your career goals:* The objective doesn't have to be written in a complete sentence. You may want to develop versions of your resume with different purpose statements so that you can personalize what you send to different companies in different industries.

- *Information about your educational accomplishments:* If you haven't yet completed your degree, write down the anticipated date: "Bachelor of Arts, May 2016." Also be sure to include any other certificates or degrees that you have earned.

- *Information about your work history:* List your most recent job first, and for each job, include the dates you worked, your position or title, the name and location of the company, and a bulleted list of your responsibilities. Describe your responsibilities using action verbs, such as *organized, developed, implemented,* and *managed.*

- *Extracurricular activities, organizations, or awards:* If you received a college scholarship, participated in a fundraising event, organized a community meeting, coached a sport, sat on a committee at your church or synagogue, or volunteered at your child's school, list these activities to demonstrate your accomplishments and contributions to society. Also be sure to list college-related accomplishments, such as making the dean's list and being a leader of or participating in student government and organizations.

- *A list of references:* As you meet and get to know people in college, consider adding their names to a list of potential references. For instance, a professor that you have gotten to know well, the advisor that you see each semester as you plan your degree, and a campus official that you have worked closely with on a project are all good candidates for writing letters of recommendation or serving as references. People you have worked with—either on the job or through a community project—are other excellent possibilities for references. Getting a person's permission before you list him or her on your resume is essential to getting a good reference.

- *A cover letter:* This letter accompanies your resume and explains in detail how your qualifications match what the employer is looking for. Like a resume, a cover letter should be brief and to the point—usually no more than a page. The more concise your resume and cover letter, the easier it will be for potential employers to determine whether you are right for the job.

As you consider what content to include in your resume, think of it as a body of evidence to support every claim you would want to make about yourself in an interview. If you believe that you are a hard-working person, then your resume should illustrate how you've managed to work during college. If you're an effective communicator, then your resume must be well written. It could also reference the high grades you've received in your composition and technical writing classes or that you participated in a high school debate team.

CASE SCENARIOS

1. Rudy is getting a degree in business management, but he doesn't have any idea how to look for a good job. In fact, he isn't really even sure if his degree is what he needs to break into financial planning, which is the career he believes will give him the financial stability that he values. Rudy has decided to use his connections with his classmates and professors to meet with a dozen different people at banks and financial institutions and to find out what it will take to get a job and succeed. It will take a few weeks to complete the interviews, but he knows that he will have time after he graduates and before he really gets serious about looking for a job.

    Use the following scale to rate the decision that has been made (1 = Poor Decision, 5 = Excellent Decision). Be prepared to explain your answer.

    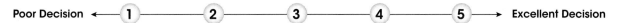

    Poor Decision ← 1 — 2 — 3 — 4 — 5 → Excellent Decision

2. Brian's dream is to own a horse farm, but he doesn't think he can afford his dream. That's why he's in his second semester as a radiology technician; it's a job with a steady income. Also, Brian doesn't want to quit school to follow his dream, because he values having an education. He realizes that as a radiology technician, he can make enough money to save up to purchase a horse farm on his own, but it will take at least 10 years of saving and planning before that will happen. Brian thinks he can endure the long hours and stressful work to make his dream come true eventually.

    Use the following scale to rate the decision that has been made (1 = Poor Decision, 5 = Excellent Decision). Be prepared to explain your answer.

    Poor Decision ← 1 — 2 — 3 — 4 — 5 → Excellent Decision

3. Lakeshia is ready to graduate with a degree in computer networking, and she has been circulating her resume with the hope that she will roll right into a job after graduation. Because Lakeshia lacks experience in this field, she has decided to elaborate on some of her responsibilities as a work study student in the information technology department and as an intern at a local advertising company. While she did provide assistance in both roles, she had few responsibilities and did not complete the kinds of projects she has listed on her resume. Lakeshia has decided to send out her resume with the exaggerations intact, because she is looking for out-of-state jobs and believes no one will find out that she's misrepresented her qualifications and experience.

    Use the following scale to rate the decision that has been made (1 = Poor Decision, 5 = Excellent Decision). Be prepared to explain your answer

    Poor Decision ← 1 — 2 — 3 — 4 — 5 → Excellent Decision

Take It with You

Action Item	Deadline	First Step
Identify potential careers that match your values, goals, and interests.		
Meet with a career counselor and some of your professors to discuss your career goals and employment strategy.		
Implement a networking strategy.		
Write your resume and review it with others.		
Practice interviewing for a job.		

REFERENCES

Bolles, R. (2011). *What color is your parachute? 2012: A practical manual for job-hunters and career-changers.* New York, NY: Ten Speed Press.

Darling, D. (2010). *The networking survival guide, second edition: Practical advice to help you gain confidence, approach people, and get the success you want,* New York, NY: McGraw Hill.

O'Brien, T. (2007). *The power of personal branding.* Los Angeles, CA: Mendham Publishing.

INDEX

Academic calendar, 19
Academic success, 2–13
    factors in, 2–6
    goal setting and, 8–11
    motivation and, 7–8
    personal values and, 6–8
    preparation and, 62
Acronyms, as study strategy, 86, 87
Acrostic sentences, as study strategy, 86, 87
Active listening, 63–64. *See also* Listening
Active reading, 74–75, 77. *See also* Reading
Administrators, relationships with/roles of, 5
Advisors, relationships with/roles of, 5
Age diversity, 98–99
Alcohol use, 122, 124–125
Art courses, note taking for, 68–69
Auditory learners. *See also* Learning styles
    assessment of, 53
    career options for, 57–58
    study strategies for, 55, 56

Back planning, as time-management
    strategy, 20
Books, costs of, 28
Boundaries, in relationships, 102–103
Brain, and theories of learning, 51
Budgets/Budgeting, 29–30

Calendars, as time-management tools, 18–19
Career counselors, 132
Career planning, 130–138
    expectations and, 130–131, 133
    goals and, 130
    guidelines for, 133
    learning styles and, 57–58
    personality and, 57–58
    strategies for, 131–138. *See also*
        Networking; Resumes
    values and, 130
Cause/Effect organization, of course
    materials, 67
Cell phones
    as distractions, 20–21, 62
    respectful use of, 22
Cheating, in college, 66, 78, 92, 113–114
Child care, 29, 84
Chronological organization, of course
    materials, 66–67
Chunking, as study strategy, 87–88
Circadian rhythms, and time management, 23
College
    costs of, 28–39, 30
    money management in, 28. *See also* Money
        management
    paying for, 32–35. *See also* Financial aid
    personal responsibility in, 3–4
    time management in, 16. *See also* Time
        management
    working during, 31. *See also* Work/Working
Communication, 96–97, 99–100
    diversity and, 96–97, 99–100, 103
    elements of, 96, 99–100
    skills in, 96
    stress and, 122
Compare/Contrast organization, of course
    materials, 67
Conflicts, 102–104
    boundaries and, 102–103
    solving of, 103–104
    in teams, 101–102
Cornell system, as note-taking strategy, 68.
    See also Note taking
Costs, of college, 28–29, 30

Counselors
    relationships with, 5
    roles of, 5, 123, 125, 132
Course materials
    organization of, 66–67, 76
    note taking from, 78–80. *See also* Note
        taking
    test content and, 89–90
Cover letters, for job applications, 136, 138.
    See also Resumes
Creative thinking
    guidelines for, 46
    problem solving and, 43
    skills in, 42, 43
Credit cards, use of, 32–33
Critical listening, 64–65. *See also* Listening
Critical reading, 74, 77. *See also* Reading
Critical thinking, 40–41
    examples of, 40–41
    guidelines for, 46
    problem solving and, 43–45
    skills in, 40–41
    test questions for, 91–92
Cultural competence, 98. *See also* Diversity
Cultural diversity, 98. *See also* Diversity

Deadlines, for assignments, 18, 75
Debit cards, use of, 33
Depression, 123, 125
Diet, and health, 63, 75, 124
Diversity, 97–99
    in college setting, 96, 97, 98, 99
    communication and, 96–97, 99–100, 103
    definition of, 97
    types of, 97–99
Documentation, of sources, 113–114
Dreams, personal, 6
Drug use, 122, 124–125
Dunn and Dunn Learning Styles Assessment, 51

Ebooks, reading of, 79
E-portfolios, 133. *See also* Resumes
Electronic calendar systems, 19. *See also*
    Calendars
Employment. *See* Career planning; Work/
    Working
Energy, and time management, 22–23
Essay questions, on tests, 92
Ethnic diversity, 98
Exams, vs. tests, 88–89. *See also* Tests
Exercise, and health, 122, 124
Expenses, as budget item, 30

Facebook, social networking via, 135
Family, support from, 5, 122–123
Fees (college), cost of, 28, 32
Fill-in-the-blank questions, on tests, 91
Final exams, 89. *See also* Tests
Financial aid, 33–35
Financial literacy, 28, 30. *See also* Money
    management
5 "Whys?" technique, 2–3
Fraud, financial, 32, 33
Friends
    as distractions, 67
    expectations of, 5
    support for/from, 5, 121, 123

Gender diversity, 97–98
Generational diversity, 98–99
Goals. *See also* Mission statement
    career planning and, 57–58
    characteristics of, 8–9

definition of, 8, 130
dreams and, 6
guidelines for, 9–10
money management and, 30–31
motivation and, 7–8
relationships and, 10
strategies for setting of, 8–10
time management and, 16
values and, 7
Grants, for college, 34–35
Groups. *See* Teams/Teamwork

Health, 124–125
    depression/suicide and, 123, 125
    diet and, 63, 75, 124
    drug and alcohol use and, 122, 124–125
    exercise and, 122, 124
    lifestyle and, 63
    sex and, 125
    sleep and, 63, 75, 122
    stress and, 121
    time management and, 22–23
Highlighting, of textbooks, 78
High school, vs. college, 3–4
History courses, note taking for, 70

Identity theft, 32–33
Income
    as budget item, 29
    diversity and, 99
Information literacy, 108–112
    definition of, 77, 108
    examples of, 108
    skills in, 108, 112
    strategies for, 109–112. *See also* Sources
Integrity
    academic standards of, 66, 78, 80, 92,
        113–114
    critical thinking and, 45
    determination and, 52
    financial fraud and, 33
    on resume, 136
    technology use and, 22
    trustworthiness and, 98, 120
    values and, 7
Intelligence, types of, 50. *See also* Learning
    styles
Internet service, cost of, 29
Internships, 132

Jobs. *See* Career planning; Work/Working

Kinesthetic learners. *See also* Learning styles
    assessment of, 50
    career options for, 57–58
    characteristics of, 53
    study strategies for, 55, 56–57

Language courses, note taking for, 69
Learning preferences, 51. *See also* Learning
    styles
Learning styles, 50–60
    assessment of, 52–54
    career planning and, 57–58
    guidelines for, 57
    intelligence and, 50
    knowledge of, 52, 57
    personality and, 51
    problem solving and, 44
    study strategies and, 52, 54–57, 65,
        66, 87
    technology and, 57
    theories of learning and, 50–51

Learning, theories of, 50–51
LinkedIn, social networking via, 135
Listening, 62–65
    active approach to, 63–64
    critical approach to, 64–65
    guidelines for, 64, 67
    note taking and. *See* Note taking
    preparing for class and, 62–63, 67
Lists, as time-management tools, 18, 19
Literature courses, note taking for, 69
Loci method, as study strategy, 86

Majors, and career options, 57–58
Matching questions, on tests, 90–91
Math courses, note taking for, 70
MBTI. *See* Myers-Briggs Type Indicator
Media use, and time management, 20–21
Memory, 85–88
    study strategies and, 85–88. *See also*
        Studying
    types of, 85
Memory Palace, as study strategy, 86
Mind maps, 56
Mission statements, 10–11, 16
Mnemonic devices, as study strategies, 85–88
Money management, 28–37
    budgeting for, 29–30
    challenges of, 28, 32–33
    goals for, 30–31
    guidelines for, 31
    knowledge about, 28–29, 30
    strategies for, 32–33
Most important/Least important organization,
    of course materials, 67
Motivation, and academic success, 7–8
Multiculturalism, 97. *See also* Diversity
Multiple-choice questions, on tests, 90
Multitasking, 22, 78
Music courses, note taking for, 69
Myers-Briggs Type Indicator (MBTI), 51

Networking, 133–136
    definition of, 133
    example of, 134
    guidelines for, 134–135
    skills in, 133–134
    types of, 134–136
Note taking, 65–70
    course/subject differences in, 68–70
    guidelines for, 66, 68–70
    learning styles and, 54–55, 65, 66
    organization of course materials and, 66–67
    preparing for class and, 62
    reading and, 76, 78–80
    strategies for, 68–70, 79–80

Objective questions, on tests, 90
Outlining, as note-taking strategy, 68, 79.
    See also Note taking

PEPS Learning Styles Inventory, 51
Personal expenses, cost of, 29
Personality
    assessment of, 51
    career planning and, 57–58
Personal responsibility
    in college, 3–4
    time management and, 16
Plagiarism, 66, 113–114. *See also* Cheating
Priorities, and time management, 16–18
Problem solving, 43–45
    approaches to, 2, 43–45
    test questions for, 91–92
Problem-solving questions, on tests, 91–92

Procrastination, and time management, 21
Professors
    conflicts with, 103–104
    learning styles of, 57
    relationships with, 5, 8, 102–103
    respect for, 22
    roles of, 5, 132

Racial diversity, 98
Reading, 74–82
    active approach to, 74–75, 77
    critical approach to, 74, 77
    guidelines for, 75, 78
    note taking and, 76, 78–80. *See also* Note
        taking
    preparation for, 74–75, 80
    skills in, 74, 76, 77
    strategies for, 76–77, 78–80
    techniques for, 76
Relationships
    boundaries for, 102–103
    conflict in. *See* Conflict
    feedback from, 11, 44
    goals and, 10, 11
    motivation and, 8
    support from, 4–6
Research papers, 111–112
Resumes, 136–138
Rhymes, as study strategy, 87
Roman room, as study strategy, 86
Room and board, cost of, 28
Roommates, support from, 5–6
Root cause analysis, 2
Routines, as time-management tools, 19–20

Scams, financial, 32, 33
Scanning, as reading technique, 76
Scholarships, college, 33–34
Science courses, note taking for, 69–70
Sex, and health, 125
Sexual orientation diversity, 97–98
Short-answer questions, on tests, 91
Skimming, as reading technique, 76
Sleep, and health, 63, 75, 122
SMART goals, 9, 31. *See also* Goals,
    characteristics of
Social media/networking, 135–136. *See also*
    Networking
Socioeconomic diversity, 99
Songs, as study strategy, 87
Sources, 109–114
    documentation of, 113–114
    evaluation of, 111–113
    finding of, 109–111
    guidelines for, 112
    technology for, 109, 112
    types of, 109–111
SQ3R, as reading strategy, 76–77
Stress, 118–123
    communication and, 122
    definition of, 118
    guidelines for, 121
    health and, 121. *See also* Health
    management of, 118, 119–123
    reactions to, 118, 119, 120, 121
    time management and, 123
Student loans, 31, 35
Studying, 84–88
    guidelines for, 84–85, 89
    learning styles and, 52, 54–57, 65, 66, 87
    note taking and. *See* Note taking
    strategies for, 52, 54–57, 65, 66, 85–88
    for tests, 84, 89. *See also* Tests
    time management and, 62, 67

Subjective questions, on tests, 90
Suicide, 123, 125
Supplies (course), cost of, 28
Syllabus/Syllabi
    assignment/course information on, 18, 62,
        65, 74, 90, 109, 123
    college cost information on, 29
    evaluation of, 40
    goal setting and, 10
    learning styles and, 51
    test information on, 90

T-system, as note-taking strategy, 68. *See also*
    Note taking
Teams/Teamwork, 100–102
Technology
    integrity in use of, 22
    learning styles and, 57
    note taking and, 78, 80
    reading and, 79
    resumes and, 133
    source searches using, 109, 112
    time management and, 20–21
Tests, 88–92
    content of, 89–90
    definition of, 88
    exams vs., 88–89
    guidelines for taking of, 89
    studying for, 84, 89. *See also* Studying
    types of, 85, 89–92
Textbooks, taking notes from, 78–80. *See also*
    Note taking
Time management, 16–25
    challenges of, 16, 20–23
    goals and, 16
    guidelines for, 20
    health and, 22–23
    mission statement and, 16
    prioritization and, 16–18
    strategies for, 16, 17–18, 20
    stress and, 123
    for studying, 62, 67
    tools for, 18–20
Transportation, cost of, 29
True/False questions, on tests, 91
Tuition, cost of, 28, 32

VAK Survey, 52–54
Values, 7, 130
Visualization, as stress-management strategy,
    121–122
Visual learners. *See also* Learning styles
    assessment of, 53
    career options for, 57–58
    characteristics of, 50
    study strategies for, 55–56

Web/Websites
    calendars on, 19
    for courses, 62
    notes available on, 66
    social networking via, 135–136
Work/Working
    applying for. *See* Resumes
    career planning and, 57–58. *See also* Career
        planning
    during college, 31, 132
    personal responsibility at, 3–4
Workspace
    characteristics of, 19
    for reading, 75
    for studying, 84
Writing, in college, 109. *See also* Research
    papers